To Achieve your Dreams
Take Control of Your
own Destiny.

Best Wishes,

Cliff Johnson

Wrong Side of the River
A Memoir by Cliff Johnson

Misty Peak Publishing
Box AL
Filer, Idaho 83328
http://www.mistypeak.com

Cover design and book typsetting by Just Your Type Desktop Publishing, San Antonio, TX (justyourtypedtp@earthlink.net)

Printed in the U.S.A.
Second Printing, February 2005

Library of Congress Control Number: 2004108414
Publisher's Cataloging-in-Publication Data
Johnson, Clifton.
        Wrong side of the river: a memoir / by Cliff Johnson.
        p. cm.
        ISBN 0-9746794-8-8

1. Johnson, Clifton – Childhood and youth. 2. Johnson, Clifton – Family.
3. Alcoholics – United States – Family Relationships. 4. Southern States – Social life and customs. 5. Texas – Biography. I. Title

CT275.J6 2004   2004108414
921–dc22

✦

Author's Disclaimer

This is a true story. Some names have been changed for reasons of privacy. The conversations that took place are not retold verbatim here, but I think my recreations give a good idea of what generally happened. I also recognize that my perceptions of what has taken place may differ from the perceptions of other family members. However, I have endeavored to tell the truth, my truth, as well as I can.

✦

ACKNOWLEDGMENTS

At the top of the list, I have to thank my loving wife, Elaine for her patience and understanding. For three years, this book received my undivided attention, leaving little time for anything else. As always, she kept me supplied with a steady flow of beverages and snacks, while offering words of encouragement. At times when even spell check didn't recognize what I was trying to spell, she was always there helping without laughing at my misguided attempts. Having the encouragement and understanding of a loving partner made writing this book possible.

My deepest appreciation goes to Sue Balcer of Just Your Type Desktop Publishing in San Antonio, Texas for the beautiful cover layout and creative interior design. It definitely sets the tone and helps relay the story I want to tell.

The little boy on the front cover is Brandon Collins of Twin Falls, Idaho. Brandon spent hours on the bridge, barefooted and cold, with three photographers relentlessly taking dozens of photos. The prize winning cover shot was taken by Brandon's Grandmother, Zandra Edwards of Twin Falls, Idaho.

I would also like to thank Angi Hargus and Colleen Wilson for their thoughtful analysis and keen eye for needed corrections in the manuscript.

A particular note of gratitude goes to my fellow members of the Idaho Writers League, and the online groups; Writing Memoir and Your Writing Choice. Many thanks for providing invaluable feedback.

✦

WRONG SIDE OF THE RIVER

A Memoir by
Cliff Johnson

CHAPTER

ONE

Bridge City Texas 1954

I could see Uncle Rudy from my perch in the top of the willow tree as he walked around the curve on Center Drive and then jumped through the cattails and over the ditch toward our backyard. The tree was a great place to check out the neighborhood and not be seen. On windy days the top would sway and I felt like the king of the world as I rocked back and forth in the salt breeze blowing in off the Gulf of Mexico. Often, I pretended I was in the crows' nest of a pirate ship, searching for a suitable location to bury my golden treasure.

I was glad Uncle Rudy didn't look up and see me. I remained motionless as he passed below, carrying his suitcase in one hand and a duffle bag in his other. A cigarette hung from the corner of his mouth, and a column of smoke shot out his nose like a dragon as he walked. If he had been one of the unsuspecting kids I was waiting for, I would have yelled "Bombs away!" and nailed him with the chinaberries and acorns I had stuffed in my pockets. Even Tarzan couldn't have blended in better, I thought to myself. He stopped in the shade of the tree directly below me, took a deep drag from his cigarette and tossed the butt in the ditch. If I was Tarzan I'd swing down on a vine and kick his butt for polluting, I chuckled to myself.

Uncle Rudy crossed our backyard without seeing me and slammed the screen door as he went in the back door of our house. I could hear him yelling at Grandma but couldn't tell what the argument was about this time. Sliding down the tree, I grabbed my Daisy BB gun that I had leaned against the fence post and darted to the corner of our house. Scooting underneath, I crawled directly under the living room and listened to their heated argument overhead.

Our house sat up on pilings about three feet off the ground, just high enough to keep out the flood waters from the hurricanes that sometimes devastated the area. I often played under the house, shielded from the scorching Texas sun. The shade kept grass from growing so that the naked dirt underneath was cool and moist; a perfect place for building toy roads, make believe mountains and hiding from fire breathing dragons.

Uncle Rudy was really my great-uncle, standing a full 6 feet 2 inches with dark eyes that matched his equally dark complexion. Compared to Grandma's small frame, he looked like a giant. The sweaty sleeveless shirts he always wore made him look macho. His body was taut and muscular. He was just as tough and strong as his job as a merchant marine in the engine room demanded. Unlike Grandma giving me an order, if he asked me to do something, I jumped to it. The look in his eyes told me he wouldn't tell me twice.

Uncle Rudy's voice drifted out the open windows along with the smell of cornbread baking. The hardwood floor creaked as he walked just above me.

"Has his mom sent any money to help out?"

I couldn't hear Grandma's answer but he spoke loud enough that I could hear every word he said.

"No, and I bet by God she won't either. Where is she living now, New York, Florida, Colorado? She doesn't stay anywhere long enough to even get mail. I would write her a damn letter myself if I knew how to get a hold of her. She's crazy if she expects you to raise the little bastard. He's been here since he was a baby and I think it's about time she started being a mom. It's not your responsibility. School will be starting soon and I think this has gone on long enough."

"Rudy, I got a letter from Cliff's mom a few weeks ago. She said that she would try and send some money to help out with his school clothes. She sent him a birthday gift, so I'm sure she's doing the best that she can."

I swallowed the lump in my throat as tears filled my eyes. I hoped Uncle Rudy didn't see the box my BB gun had arrived in. Mom had sent it just a few days before, and I'm sure Uncle Rudy would have something bad to say about that too, if he knew. Grandma had pointed to the Los Angeles postmark stamped on the box when it arrived. Mom had sent me new shoes too, so he had no right to say she wasn't helping out. I hated him being home and wished he would just stay on his stupid ship. With him home again, he would be sleeping in my room and I would be forced to sleep on the couch. He told me it was his room, but it had been mine for as long as I could remember. Just because he helped Grandma buy the house and had it moved from the Navy base in Orange, Texas after the war, he thought that gave him special privileges.

School would be starting in another week, and I would be entering the first grade. Some of my friends were excited about going to school, but I wasn't. No way! I would be expected to wear those dang shoes all day, and I dreaded the thought of that. It was bad enough to have to wear them to church on Sunday mornings.

Just last Saturday, Grandma and I had gone to Beaumont with some of her church friends to outfit me with clothes and school supplies. I saw the stress written on her face when the clerk rang up the bill. The strain of having to raise me meant another mouth to feed and tested her already tight budget, and now, to add to her problems Uncle Rudy had to show up. Obviously he was drinking again and Grandma always hated that.

I was still in my hiding spot under the house, but could hear Uncle Rudy's gruff voice above me.

"How much money did you give to that damn church this month? I've got half a notion to go down and tell that lazy ass preacher what I think of him, begging money from an old lady. You don't even have enough money to take care of yourself, much less give the shit away like it grows on a damn tree."

It sounded like Grandma's voice was coming out the kitchen window so I crawled closer to listen.

"Rudy, you know I don't like it when you start in on my church. We're getting by just fine," Grandma responded confidently.

"Only because I send you half of the goddamn money I make," he yelled.

I could barely hear Grandma's answer but could tell by her voice that she was crying.

"Rudy, I wish you wouldn't use the Lord's name in vain. You know I don't like that."

"Well you can just wish in one hand and shit in the other and see which one fills up first. You wouldn't have a pot to piss in if it wasn't for me. I work my ass off for months at a time only to come home and put up with this bullshit."

The heavy footsteps above told me Uncle Rudy was walking toward the door. I scooted back further into the shadows to make sure he didn't see me. A black widow spider crawled on the floor joist just above me, and I crushed it into a sticky blob with the barrel of my BB gun. The screen door slammed again and I could see his oil covered black boots as he stomped down the wooden steps. It would be easy to grab his ankle and make him fall. I held my breath as he walked past the side of the house and kicked my rusted Tonka truck, tumbling out of his way.

Skippy, my black Labrador puppy was tied to a fig tree by the corner of the house. I had named her Skippy because we both liked that brand of peanut butter. She ran to meet Uncle Rudy, wagging her tail. If he kicked her, he was going to be so sorry. My BB gun was cocked and ready to fire. The bottom of his butt was dead-centered in my peep sight. I could bounce BB's off Grandma's galvanized flower watering can at 100 feet or shoot mosquito hawks off the clothesline and very seldom missed, so he better watch his step. Fighting the urge to pull the trigger anyway, I didn't make a sound. I stayed hidden in the shadows as he hopped the ditch in front of the house and started walking down Turner Drive toward the highway.

When I knew Uncle Rudy was out of sight, I went into the house to check on Grandma. She was folding clothes and tried to ignore me, acting like she didn't hear me come in. A tear ran from the corner of her eye and continued down her cheek. She wiped it away, trying to keep me from seeing it. We were close and I could feel her pain. I was sorry he yelled at her because of me. She had raised me since my Mom left me there when I was three years old.

"Sometimes he just makes me so angry I could shake him," Grandma blurted out.

She turned her head so I wouldn't see her crying, but I could tell she was upset. Uncle Rudy was always unpleasant to be around and seemed to disagree with anything Grandma did or said. I know he resented his mother having to raise me, but that wasn't our fault. My adventuresome spirit didn't do much to help matters either.

Uncle Rudy's job took him to countries all over the world, so Grandma and I didn't see him but once or twice each year. Even that was too often for me. When he was off the ship, he would hang out in the bars on Proctor Street in Port Arthur, Texas. He bragged that some of the places were so rough if you didn't have a knife when you went in, they would give you one. If he came home, (many nights he didn't) he'd be drunk and boisterous. It was almost like he wanted to fight and was just waiting for someone to say the wrong thing to set him off. Sometimes I watched him if he wasn't looking, and studied his ruggedness. He always seemed very serious and demanding, but never particularly happy to be home. It was as though something was missing in his life. Grandma thought he needed Jesus, but I thought he just needed a home somewhere else.

The last time Uncle Rudy was home, he came in late one night, drunk and crying. He woke Grandma up, insisting she pray for him. He told us in detail how one of his shipmates had gone crazy miles from land and climbed the mast of his ship, all the way to the very top. Some of the men were trying to talk him down when he yelled; "If birds can fly—so can I." The man dove straight out from the mast, flapping his arms like the wings of a bird all the way down to the ship's iron deck where he landed face down with a bone crunching thud. Uncle Rudy had to help with the gruesome task of cleaning up the mess.

CHAPTER
TWO

I t had been raining all evening and was well after dark by the time Uncle Rudy came home again. I was ready for bed and sat on the couch staring at the motion lamp on the end table. The lamps inner lining turned slowly, depicting a roaring forest fire with a waterfall in the foreground and animals running for safety from the flames.

Uncle Rudy sat down in the overstuffed chair next to the lamp. The moisture on his skin reflected the flickering red light as the lamp slowly turned, making him look like a picture of the devil himself. Grandma's voice broke the trance the lamp had placed on me.

"Cliff, lay down and get to sleep. You need to start going to bed earlier or your going to have a hard time getting up for school."

I wished that Uncle Rudy had just stayed in one of the hotels in Port Arthur so I could sleep in my own bed. Some of the bars there had rooms above them where he usually stayed. Actually it would have been nice if he had gone to the amusement park on Pleasure Pier. I smiled at the thought of Uncle Rudy being stuck there for the night when the bridge over the Inter-coastal Canal closed for the night. All the mosquitoes on the island would die from alcohol poisoning. I smiled at that thought and it caught Uncle Rudy's attention.

"What the hell are you smiling about?" Uncle Rudy's voice boomed, jarring me back to reality and spilled over the images in my mind.

"Nothing," I answered quickly, trying hard to cover my thoughts.

"Don't lie to me boy. I know there had to be some devious thought going through your little pea-brain. Now I want to know what you were smiling about."

"I was just thinking how much fun it would be to go to Pleasure Pier and ride the roller coaster," I lied.

I could tell Uncle Rudy was drunk by the way he talked and smelled. His dark angry eyes followed my every move. To avoid eye contact, I looked at his big work-hardened hands, and watched the ashes from his cigarette as they dropped to the hardwood floor. From the hard look he gave me, I could tell he saw me watching his cigarette. His eyes followed mine back to the motion lamp. It was almost like he could read my mind. Yes, I did wonder if he was going to catch the house on fire. He wasn't careful with his cigarettes and he had caught his bed on fire one time when he was drunk.

"Cliff." My stare at the motion lamp was again interrupted by his voice.

"Yes Sir," I answered, wondering what I had done.

"You wanna go alligator hunting?"

"Sure — when can we go?" I answered in amazement. He had never asked me to do anything with him before.

Grandma had a frown followed by a look of disbelief on her face.

"Get your shirt back on, we're going right now."

"Rudy, it's raining and he's ready for bed. Why don't you wait and do it another time? At least wait until morning," Grandma pleaded.

Grandma positioned herself behind Uncle Rudy and whispered for me not to go.

He noticed her shaking her head from side to side and exploded in an angry rage; "We're going — that's all there is too it."

"But Rudy," Grandma was almost begging.

"But nothing — damn it!" he shouted. Red-faced, the arteries throbbed in his neck, and his eyes bounced in anger. He turned toward me with his fists doubled up like he wanted to hit someone.

"Do you want to go, Cliff?" he asked, looking directly at me as if I might change my mind.

The pressure was on and the room silent as they both stood there looking at me and waiting for an answer. Uncle Rudy's brow creased with anticipation. The look on his face told me I better say yes or there would be big trouble. It was decision time. Uncle Rudy would take his rage out on both of us if I changed my mind. Maybe it would be best to just agree to go, I surmised. I didn't want to answer, but they both stood there waiting. His eyes were locked on mine in a cold glare like a king cobra ready to strike with deadly force.

"Well—uh, yeah I guess," I answered, still unsure if I had made the right decision.

With a slight smile and a flood of foul-smelling breath, Uncle Rudy bellowed at me to hurry up and get dressed. It was too late to change my mind now. Grandma was still trying to talk him out of going but he insisted.

"Cliff wants to do this, and by God we were going, come hell or high water."

His demanding nature would have it no other way. A little rain isn't going to stop an alligator hunt. After all; "We are men," he reminded me with a slight smile.

Chapter THREE

I had been to Cow Bayou many times before, but not in the direction we were going and never at night. I always followed the oyster shell covered road, and crossed the cattle guard if the Brahma bulls weren't in sight. It would have been easier to go that way, but for some reason Uncle Rudy wanted to follow the canal. Maybe he's afraid of the bulls, I reasoned.

The thought of him being afraid made me wonder if he would be brave enough to catch an alligator if we found one. I would have never thought that he was afraid of anything. I had been chased up a tree by the bulls more than once, and it was no big deal. Maybe it wasn't the bulls at all. Maybe he thought we would find an alligator along the way if we stayed close to the canal. That had to be the only logical explanation.

The light drizzle created a dreamlike mist as Uncle Rudy led the way down the overgrown canal bank, clearing a path with his body as we went. The dark color of the water made me wonder where the alligators were hiding. Hordes of mosquitoes hung motionless inches above the water, and then moved in unison at our approach looking for an easy meal of warm blood.

As we neared Cow Bayou the moon broke through the dark clouds allowing the trees along the bank to cast their shadows across the murky water. Cypress knees stuck up from the ground like upside down icicles. As I studied their form it reminded me of the ghost of Jean Lafitte and his band of pirates watching over their treasure. Like silent sentinels, they stood there never uttering a sound. Patches of mist rose above the water and moved with the breeze like a hundred ghosts waving at us to join them. Spanish moss waving in the breeze dangled almost to the ground from the trees. My friends and I had nick-named it witch's hair because its gray, threadlike stems drooped in long, matted clusters like a witch having a bad hair day.

It seemed like we had been walking for hours, but it was probably closer to thirty minutes. The brush and sticker vines were dripping from the light rain and mist, soaking my clothes as I brushed against them. Uncle Rudy used a flashlight to wipe a spider web out of the way, as a big three-inch Banana Spider dropped to the ground at our feet. Once in a while he would let a willow branch swing back and hit me across the face with enough force to bring tears to my eyes. It hurt but I had to be tough. I didn't want Uncle Rudy to think I couldn't keep up. I couldn't help but wonder if he was doing it on purpose. His words: *We are men*, kept ringing in my ears.

Fear made me apprehensive, yet I was eager to keep going. This was the most exciting adventure I had ever experienced, and I couldn't wait to tell my friends.

What if we caught a gator and brought it home with us? Now that would be something to brag about to everyone! I could already picture my friends and the neighbors gathered in our back yard, looking at our alligator tied to a tree. Maybe I could charge them all a quarter. Then again, what if the gator caught us? That thought caused me to shiver in my wet clothes, and I tried to fight off the chill that ran through my body.

The bayou is a dark and scary place for anyone, especially in the middle of the night. I was in awe but knew the bayou could be deadly. Grandma had told me how her brother had almost lost an arm while trying to catch an alligator on Cow Bayou, back when he was a teenager. Her story was not what I wanted to be thinking about, but considering what we were doing, it was hard to forget.

I had no idea how Uncle Rudy planned to catch an alligator if we saw one. We didn't have a rope or anything to shoot it with, but I guessed the answer to my question would come if we found one. Too bad I couldn't have brought my BB gun.

"Where are the alligators?" I whispered, almost afraid I'd scare them off, but secretly hoping I would.

Uncle Rudy didn't answer, but raised his arm and pointed across the water toward the cypress trees on the distant bank. I strained my eyes but could only see the outline of the trees.

"We have to swim across the bayou to that island to catch one," he whispered without looking at me. He seemed to be in a trance with his eyes fixed on the dark water.

"But I don't know how to swim," I protested.

"I'll help you — now come on. We didn't come this far for you to turn into a baby and want to go home. Don't puss out now!"

My body was consumed with fear and I couldn't stop shaking. I crossed my arms and hugged myself in an attempt to stop trembling, but it didn't help. I had never been so afraid in my life.

Uncle Rudy's hard callused hands grabbed my arm and pulled me into the dark waters of the bayou. Trying with all my might, I struggled to pull free from his grasp to no avail. Within just a few feet the water was over my head. I begged Uncle Rudy to stop as I hung onto his shirt and fought to stay afloat.

My heart practically leaped out of my chest as Uncle Rudy grabbed me with his other hand and pushed my head under the cold water. I struggled to pull free but his grip on my arm only tightened. With both hands he pushed me to the bottom and then attempted to stand on top of me. Pulling on his legs didn't seem to make any difference. I was fighting for my life and it was obvious he was trying to drown me. There was nothing I could do but hold my breath and continue to struggle with all my strength.

CHAPTER FOUR

I couldn't understand why Uncle Rudy was doing this to me. I tried to get free by rolling out from under him, but he was walking on top of me as if I were the log in a log rolling contest.

Fortunately, the bayou bottom was muddy and as I rolled, I was getting covered with thick, black, bayou mud. The muddy water stung my eyes and I couldn't see. Uncle Rudy lost his balance and fell backwards, giving me time to surface for air. As I scrambled toward the shore he tackled me from behind. Confused and crying, I begged him to stop but my cries were ignored.

Without answering Uncle Rudy pushed me back under the murky water. This time he knelt down on top of me with all his weight, forcing me into the muddy bottom. Struggling to stay alive, my left foot found solid ground and I pulled out from under him again. This time I came up behind him in deeper water. He lunged toward me, but I dog-paddled and kicked away from him as fast as I possibly could. With each passing moment the distance between us grew. My arms felt as if they were made of lead, but I refused to give up.

Uncle Rudy was having difficulty standing on the slick bottom and fell toward me. I was terrified and the adrenaline shot my heart rate to full speed. Overcome with panic, I could feel my chest pounding like a drum ready to burst. Dog-paddling even faster toward the center of the bayou, I could hear Uncle Rudy calling from behind.

"Cliff, you better get your ass back here if you don't want the gators to eat you. You're making a big mistake."

Behind me lay inescapable death with Uncle Rudy yelling for me to come back. Ahead of me lay uncharted dark, murky waters of the bayou and nocturnal-hunting creatures. I was exhausted and knew I couldn't make it across the bayou but I had to try. I feared my thrashing around in the water would attract the alligators, and that would be a horrible way to die. My situation just grew worse with each passing moment.

"God please help me," I prayed, as I fought to stay afloat.

Between my prayer and the ones that Grandma was surely saying at home, a miracle took place. This stretch of Cow Bayou didn't normally have much current, but I was being swept downstream away from Uncle Rudy. I felt a renewed strength build in my body knowing I was going to make it to safety. A sense of peace underlying what was happening surged through me.

Uncle Rudy struggled through the underbrush to keep up, but the distance between us was growing. Like a mighty river, the current carried me out of his sight, and then like magic, delivered me close enough to the bank that I was able to make it to shore.

Pulling myself up on the roots of a cypress tree, I tried to stand but my legs felt limp and rubbery. I could still hear Uncle Rudy crashing through the brush and calling my name.

Confused, I ran blindly into the darkness breaking through

curtains of spider-webs, wiping them from my face as I ran. The worry of getting a snake or spider bite wasn't even a concern at this point. I wasn't even sure if I was running in the right direction to find home.

Uncle Rudy's voice still echoed behind me.

"Cliff, you're really starting to piss me off! You get your ass back here right now! Do you hear me? I mean it—you get back here right now, damn it!"

I continued to stumble and fall as he chased me through the tangled brush into the dark and ominous swamp. He must have lost the flashlight or he would be using it to search the darkness for me.

I stopped to catch my breath and froze in silence for a long moment, trying to decide which direction to go. All I could hear was the buzz of mosquitoes and the roar of blood pulsating in my ears.

Just when I hoped it was safe to rest, I heard dead tree branches snapping behind me. Studying the pitch-black, I thought I could see his silhouette in the darkness and remained still. The silence that followed was profound except for my teeth chattering so loud, I was afraid he would hear them. I thought of hiding in the bushes along the canal, but what if he found me? He would probably just drown me right there. I wished I could be swallowed by the darkness and just stay hidden, but I didn't feel safe staying where I was. I had to keep moving or he would find me. I picked up my pace and started running even faster into the night.

Water splashed in the canal as I ran along the bank, driving my imagination wild with possibilities. Could it be an alligator? Everything was so confusing—so overwhelming. I wasn't even sure where I was or if I was running in the right direction. It was too dark to see what lay ahead of me, but I knew what was behind and slowing down would mean my death. I couldn't let Uncle Rudy catch sight of me, as I'm sure he could outrun me with his long legs.

A loud pop underneath my foot, and the smell that followed, told me I had stepped on a rotten egg. I had heard that alligators guard their eggs. I hoped it was a goose or duck nest, but I didn't slow down long enough to find out. The stench of the rotten egg seemed to float on the light wings of the midnight wind, following me as I ran. I worried the smell alone might lead Uncle Rudy my direction.

Open ground and lights visible through the thick brush gave me a burst of energy. I charged full speed ahead but was brought to a teeth jarring halt by a barbed wire fence. I was knocked backwards and landed in the thorns of a blackberry bush. The sting caused me to cry out loud, but only slowed me down long enough to dive under the bottom strand of wire. I could feel blood oozing from the raised welts on my chest and stomach as I ran across the pasture.

Blinded by tears, I could make out the lights to our house in the distant. My side ached from running but I couldn't slow down. I kept looking over my shoulder expecting Uncle Rudy to be gaining, and wondering if he would pop out of the darkness in front of me.

Skippy started barking as I ran into our yard and cleared the front steps with one jump. Bursting into the house out of breath I gasped for air and tried to talk, but the words just wouldn't come. My whole body shook uncontrollably.

"Thank God you're okay! What in the world is going on?" Grandma cried out with a look of concern on her wrinkled face. I tried to talk slow and tell her what Uncle Rudy had done, but the words spilled out so fast she made me stop and start over. My clothes were wet, torn, and covered with mud. My body burned from the cuts caused by the barbed wire and sticker bushes. Scrapes and bruises covered my body but I was just thankful to be alive.

Grandma rushed me into her bedroom in case Uncle Rudy came in. With a wet wash cloth she cleaned my wounds, and reminded me she had tried to talk me out of going in the first place. I needed to start listening to her. Sternly she told me to never go anywhere with Uncle Rudy again. I nodded in agreement. My life depended on it.

Grandma made a pallet for me to sleep on in her room and had me cleaned up and tucked in before Uncle Rudy came stumbling through the door. I could hear him through the closed bedroom door, cussing and arguing with Grandma. He told her how I had fallen into the bayou and lied about how he had jumped in to save me. I would have surely died if he hadn't made it to me in time. He didn't have any idea why I ran when he was only trying to help me. I wanted to come out of the bedroom and say what really happened, but I was paralyzed with fear. All I could do was lay still and hope he didn't come in the bedroom. His deep voice caused a cold shiver to run up my spine. I eyed the bedroom window as a possible escape route just in case.

Crawling to the closet at the foot of Grandma's bed, I removed my BB gun that she had draped a dress over. She was probably afraid Uncle Rudy would snoop around while he was home and discover it. I moved it under Grandma's bed beside me, just in case I needed to defend myself during the night.

I fell asleep before Grandma came to bed but awoke from a nightmare sometime during the night. My body was covered with perspiration. The nightmare seemed so real. Uncle Rudy had been sitting on top of me, trying to remove my tonsils with a fish hook and a piece of string. A sense of relief overcame me when I realized it was just a dream.

Somehow it all seemed so distant...almost as if it had been someone else's life that almost ended. My sore throat reminded me of the bayou water I had swallowed earlier. The aches in my body and the welts on my arms were a vivid reminder that the dream was based on real memories of him trying to kill me. I moved my pallet closer to Grandma's bed and laid awake for hours with one hand on the BB gun, my mind still racing. I knew I wouldn't be forgetting this night.

Thoughts flowed through my mind like a rushing river. What if he came into the room and killed me while I was sleeping? Maybe I should just kill him first...but how? Grandma had the keys for the Turner Cemetery, a small private cemetery in Bridge City that our ancestors had started years ago. We could bury him there, and I would be more than glad to dig his grave. Visions of Uncle Rudy loaded in my wagon as I pulled him down Morning Glory Drive to the cemetery flowed through my mind. He was really too big for the wagon. His arms and legs would probably drag on the ground, but with help from my friends we could find a way to get him there.

As the endless possibilities played through my brain, I thought out each scenario and why it wouldn't work. My BB gun would only make him mad. If I shot him in the eyes, he wouldn't be able to find me. What if I hit him in the head with a hammer while he was sleeping? Would it kill him? I could almost visualize the hammer hitting his hard head and bouncing off, then his big hand grabbing my arm. I shuddered at the thought of him using the hammer on me. Hours later, I drifted off to sleep but continued to have nightmares about him.

When I woke the next morning, Grandma was already in the other room. I lay on the floor and listened for Uncle Rudy's voice but couldn't hear him. Quietly, I crawled to the bedroom door and placed my ear up to it, but I still couldn't hear his voice. Maybe he was still sleeping. The aroma of Seaport Coffee wafted under the door and reminded me that Grandma seldom made coffee just for herself. If Uncle Rudy was awake, he sure wasn't saying anything.

Grandma heard the bedroom door creak as I peeked out.

"It's okay; he left first thing this morning,"

"When will he be back?" I asked.

"He catches his ship this afternoon, so it will be a long time," she replied.

"That's fine with me; I hope he never comes back," I replied grudgingly.

The frown on Grandma's face told me I had said the wrong thing. I wondered if I had talked out loud while I was dreaming, and Grandma had heard me plotting to kill Uncle Rudy. "Cliff, come here and sit down—we need to talk." I moved to the sofa, concerned with Grandma's unfamiliar scowl.

"Your Uncle Rudy is very sorry for what happened last night, and he asked me to pray for him this morning. If he hadn't been drinking none of this would have happened. He promised me that he would try his hardest to stop drinking. He knows it's ruining his life. The devil wants to destroy him, but I know the Lord won't let it happen if we just keep praying for him. Now Cliff, you have to remember and accept this; God has forgiven him and you need to do the same."

I didn't say anything but nodded my head in agreement.

Conversation of his trying to drown me never came up again after that morning. It was buried like a lot of other secrets that stayed deeply hidden within the confines of our family, never to be talked about, ever. Just like why my Mom had left me at my Great Grandmother's all these years. Burning questions like, who my dad was or where he lived. Secrets that were just as dark as the bayou itself.

With Uncle Rudy back on the ship, everything soon returned to normal. A summer's collection of mud was washed away from my tough bare feet and I would start the first grade at Bridge City Elementary in a week. Grandma often joked that I was born with webs between my toes just like a duck. The first time she said that, I looked to see if it was true and she almost fell off the chair laughing.

Sarah Simmons was a cute little freckle-faced girl who lived just down the road from us. She had the heart and soul of a tomboy and wasn't a girly-girl, like some of the girls I knew from church and school. A seasoned professional at the education process and its rules, Sarah would be entering the second grade. She had warned me ahead of time about the schools "shoe requirement." She was both a girl and a friend, but if anyone would have suggested she was my girlfriend, they would have probably been on the receiving end of a bloody nose or black eye.

Like most hot Saturday afternoons, I found my way to the ditch behind our house. Staying low, I waded my way downstream behind Aunt Lillie's house. Aunt Lillie is my Great-Aunt. If she told Grandma I was playing in the mud again, I would be in deep trouble.

Weighing the chances of Aunt Lillie seeing me, I decided to risk it and go skinny dipping. Avoiding the thorns that grew along the ditch bank, I hung my clothes on a willow branch and carefully made my way into the water.

Mosquito hawks took flight and hummed above my head like tiny helicopters. A group of minnows darted for the safety of deep water, their shiny bodies wiggling and reflecting the sun like miniature mirrors. The mud felt cool as it squished up between my toes and coated my legs. A crawfish scurried backwards away from my feet with its claws open in the attack position and disappeared in a cloud of mud.

I moved cautiously into the deeper water, surveying any danger. The need to get wet in the hot Texas sun far outweighed the dangers of an occasional eel or snake. That was the last thing I wanted to see, but I kept my eyes peeled just in case.

With each step, I sank deeper into the mud. The water was cool toward the bottom, but the upper half was heated by the scorching sun. Walking down the middle, my body plowed a small wake of water that rushed to both banks. Breaking the utter stillness of mid-afternoon, turtles dove in the water with a splash. I gently pushed lily pads aside and chased a bull frog as it swam with grace. If I could catch a frog, Grandma would be pleased. She often said nothing tasted as good as fried frog legs.

The ditch was shallow, with only a few feet of water, but still deep enough to allow me to crawl along the bottom. The frog was still swimming about ten feet in front of me, but I was getting closer. With my eyes just above the surface, I pretended to be an alligator. Digging my hands into the squishy mud like alligator's feet, I pulled myself along the bottom, about to catch my next meal. A cardinal sitting on the weeds overhanging the ditch bank flew off in panic as I passed underneath, almost close enough to reach up and touch. As I closed the gap on the frog it disappeared under the surface and escaped sure death.

When the ditch became too shallow to move ahead, I stood up and started walking, sinking knee deep into the mud with each step.

The areas of my body covered with mud felt cool. I purposely added more, until my entire body was covered. The sizzling sun quickly baked the thin layers I had smeared on myself and caused the mud to crack as it dried. Filling each fracture like a talented sculptor, I worked the mud smooth until I developed a walking masterpiece.

I wondered what I looked like: an alligator or a walking-mud-monster. Whatever I was, I looked really good and needed a second opinion. When a person looks that great, you really have to show someone. Aunt Lillie wouldn't be a good choice and definitely not Grandma. I was starting to develop a dislike for Grandma's willow switches.

The only person I could think of whom would appreciate my artistic skill was Sarah Simmons. I knew if she saw me this way she would think it was funny. Climbing up the ditch bank, I decided to pay her a visit. If I tried to put my clothes on, I would have to bend over and some of the mud would crack and fall off. Besides, I figured I had enough mud covering me that no one would be able to tell if I was a boy or girl anyway. With my arms held straight out from my body, I walked stiff-legged to her house like a mummy fresh from the tomb. Too bad it wasn't Halloween.

Proudly, I knocked on her door with nothing on but dried gray mud and a big wide smile. Mr. Simmons answered the door and jumped back with a shocked look on his face. I could tell I was in deep trouble. He apparently didn't think I looked funny at all. I could see Sarah at the kitchen table snapping green beans with her mom and sister.

"Can Sarah come out and play?" I asked unashamed, knowing what Mr. Simmons answer would be from the fire in his eyes.

Grabbing my arm, he spun me around and pushed me toward the front steps.

"Get the hell out of here and don't you ever come back again, you little bastard!" His foot caught me in the butt as I jumped ahead.

Yikes! This was the first time I had ever been cussed at by anyone other than Uncle Rudy. Boy, was he angry.

I glanced back as I headed down their driveway and saw Sarah and the rest of her family looking out the window. Mrs. Simmons was shaking her head, but it looked like Sarah was laughing as the curtain closed. At least she got to see how good I looked from behind. I felt a slight draft as I walked back to the canal and noticed a patch of mud was missing where he kicked me. Some people just don't have a sense of humor.

Mr. Simmons was probably still mad from a few weeks before, when he came home and found tomato ketchup smeared on his front door. When he cornered me in his yard, I tried to convince him that a big cowboy and Indian battle had taken place while they were gone. He just wouldn't buy that story and made me scrub the mess off his door.

Mrs. Simmons always blamed me for peeing in her steam iron too, but I swear it wasn't me. Actually, I think their dog did it. Once you get branded as a little bastard, it seems like you get blamed for everything that happens in the neighborhood, whether you're responsible or not.

It was a long time before Sarah was allowed to play with me again, and it was even longer before I went back to her house when her dad was home. Mr. Simmons just never seemed to forget my muddy visit that day and frowned each time he saw me.

Chapter SIX

Verna, my Mom's little sister, arrived in Bridge City just in time for Halloween. Verna's dad moved to Houston after his divorce, and like Uncle Rudy, he too had a serious drinking problem. Verna had lived with her dad for almost two years, but ran away from home each time they had an argument. She would bounce back and forth between her mom and dad, but this was the first time she came to stay with us.

Though Verna is my Aunt, I just call her Verna because she is only six years older than me. All my friends think she looks like a Hollywood movie star and she often dresses the part.

Verna's short dresses caused Grandma to squirm with protest.

"Verna, I wish you would wear something else. What if Aunt Lillie or the neighbors see you dressed like that?" Grandma would frown.

"The Lord only knows what everyone must think."

Verna's hair was dyed blonde, and she walked with a wiggle. Other people's opinions didn't seem to bother her. Everywhere we went; men stared at her, while women turned up their noses, shaking their heads in disgust. We quickly grew very close, with her assuming both roles of big sister and mom, all rolled into one. In spite of the gossiping old ladies, I felt proud being seen with her.

On Halloween night, Verna taught me the fine art of "trick-or-treating" in a big way. She dressed as Marilyn Monroe and looked just like her. I wanted to be a mud monster, but Verna didn't think it would be a good idea. Instead, I used an old bed sheet with eye holes cut out and became a regular old boring ghost. We made the rounds pulling my old red wagon with nails bent on the axles to keep the wheels from falling off. A large cardboard "candy" box fit perfectly in the back, and we knocked on every door in Bridge City.

About 9:30 p.m., we took our load of candy home and started over, knocking on the same doors again. Sometime after 11:00 p.m. people became unfriendly, and several expressed it was time for us to go home. The houses where no one answered still received the dreaded "soaping of the windows treatment" despite the fact they'd given earlier.

Even the Piggly-Wiggly store didn't have a supply of candy like we had.

When Christmas season arrived, Verna decided we needed a Christmas tree. Maybe if Grandma had a car, we would have driven north to the woods to cut one, but transportation was a luxury we didn't have.

Grandma had often told us that our ancestors had planted all the oak trees in Bridge City when she was a little girl. Verna reasoned that if our ancestors planted the oak trees, then they probably planted all the pine trees too. Besides, being native Texans should entitle us to any tree we wanted.

The nicest pine tree in all of Bridge City was on Mr. Trahan's property, just a short distance from our house. I think Verna knew the Trahan's probably wouldn't agree that the tree was really ours, so she thought it best to cut it down in the dark of the night.

Verna knew I doubted her logic about the tree being ours. "Look Cliff, I'll prove it's all right if you're worried about it," Verna whispered. "Then why are you whispering?" That question caused Verna to frown at me.

"Grandma, can I use your Bible? I want to show Cliff something I read one time." Grandma seemed pleased as she handed Verna her old bible and we sat down at the table to study. I'm sure Grandma thought all those years of praying for us were paying off. Grandma smiled as she said goodnight, went to the bedroom and closed her door.

I grew impatient as Verna went through page after tattered page of the Bible. After searching for ten or fifteen minutes, her face lit up when she found what she was looking for. "It's right here," she whispered. "Why are you whispering?" I asked again. "Because we don't want to wake Grandma, that's why. Now listen to what it says right here; Deuteronomy 23:24 'When thou comest into thy neighbor's vineyard, then thou mayest eat grapes thy fill at thine own pleasure; but thou shalt not put any in thy vessel.' 23:25 'When thou comest into the standing corn of thy neighbor, then thou mayest pluck the ears with thine hand; but thou shalt not move a sickle unto thy neighbor's standing corn.'

"So just think about it Cliff, Christmas is about Jesus' birthday, right?" I nodded my head in agreement. "If it is okay to take your neighbor's grapes and corn, do you really think Jesus would care if we took a tree to celebrate his birthday?"

Still having some doubt, I shrugged my shoulders. It made some sense, but it wasn't Jesus I was worried about. It was the welts Grandma's willow switches would leave across my butt if she found out.

Verna and I walked hunched over along Mr. Trahan's fence line, then crawled into their yard, dragging an old crosscut handsaw we had taken from our shed. We could see Mr. Trahan sitting in a chair reading, while his wife appeared busy in the kitchen. A dry west wind made it a bit warmer than usual for a Texas winter night. The Trahan's living room window was wide open, with only a window screen holding back the horde of mosquitoes that were eating us alive. We were close enough to their open window that we could hear Cajun accordion music coming from their record player. I recognized the song as "Jole Blonde" and could hear Mr. Trahan singing along with the music. We couldn't help but snicker at how loud and off key he was. I couldn't understand a word he was singing, but it had a nice sound.

Taking turns, we pulled the saw back and forth to the beat of the music.

"Verna, can I ask you something?"

"What?" she whispered.

"What's a sickle?"

"What?"

"You know—a sickle, like the story you read from the Bible."

"Cliff, just shut up before they hear us, and keep sawing!"

It must have taken half an hour before the tree toppled with a crash that got Mr. Trahan's attention. The music stopped. He rushed out the door and stood on the front steps looking around. We lay motionless on the ground behind our twenty foot tree. I wanted so badly to run, but Verna held me back.

"Don't move," she whispered.

I had a sick feeling in my stomach and felt like praying, but somehow that didn't seem right. All this to celebrate Jesus' birthday!

After the longest three minutes of my life, Mr. Trahan went back inside. Verna and I waited patiently until the music started again. The tree looked much larger lying on the ground. When we discovered it was too heavy to drag, she decided we only needed the top six feet. It didn't take near as long to cut that section in two, and we quickly made our getaway dragging our trophy along the fence behind us.

The next morning when Grandma discovered the huge Christmas tree in our living room, I graciously let Verna do all the explaining. Grandma listened with an inquisitive look.

"We walked down to Cow Bayou and found it growing there," she lied. Grandma looked at me. I just nodded, but added: "And it was dark and scary too." Verna smiled at me for adding such a nice finishing touch to her story. She told a much better lie than I could have. If Grandma had known the truth, she would have stripped the willow tree of all the switches and probably went to the neighbors for more. Sometimes I wondered if my ancestors had planted the willow trees too. Maybe they just planned ahead so Grandma would always have a fresh switch supply to use on future generations.

When Mr. Trahan discovered his tree missing, he had to know it was someone in the neighborhood who had taken it. It wouldn't have taken too much detective work to have tracked us down by the trail of pine needles we left behind. Being almost Christmas, possibly the Trahan's knew we took the tree, but decided we needed it more than they did.

The tree and our secret were safe within the walls of our house, but after Christmas a new problem presented itself. Grandma took the ornaments off and put them away for another year.

"Cliff, would you please drag the Christmas tree out back and put it by the trash barrel?"
I cringed at the thought, as Mr. Trahan was outside working on his car. With a clear view of our back yard, I knew he would see me dragging the tree. If Verna were home, I'm sure she would know how to handle this, but she was working as a carhop at the drive-in.

"Grandma, I don't feel very good right now. Can I take it out later?" I asked, hoping I could stall her until after dark or at least until Mr. Trahan wasn't outside.

"No, you can do it now and take a nap when you're done. I want to get this house cleaned up," she answered.

"But Grandma," I whimpered. It didn't work. She stood there with her hands on her hips and I was forced to face my doom in the back yard.

As quietly as possible, I pulled the tree outside as Grandma held the screen door open. Crossing the backyard, I avoided looking toward Mr. Trahan and deposited the tree near our rusted out burn barrel. As I turned and started walking back towards my house, Mr. Trahan yelled for me to wait. My heart froze. He was walking across the field toward me in a fast pace. My first instinct was to run, but he would probably just come to my house. What would I say if he asked me about the tree? My legs were shaking and I couldn't stop them. I could feel the blood drain from my face as I stopped and turned to face him.

"What?" I asked, embarrassed to look him in the face.

"Where did you get that Christmas tree, Cliff?"

The story of George Washington and the cherry tree flashed through my mind. I struggled with the question for a moment; but quickly recovered. "Uh—I —uh, I think Verna got it down by Cow Bayou somewhere," I stuttered, my palms sweating.

"You know your Uncle Rudy and I are friends. I think I need to talk to him about this when he gets home. You know why?" he asked.

"No sir," I answered, still avoiding his gaze.

"Because that tree looks exactly like the one that was growing in my yard before someone cut it down last week."

"He should be home any day now," I said with as much courage as I could muster. If Mr. Trahan told Uncle Rudy, he would kill me for sure. Mr. Trahan stormed off mad and now I had something else to worry about.

CHAPTER
SEVEN

Grandma asked me to go to the store for her about once a week. Usually her friends from church would take her shopping but it always seemed like she would forget something and send me. I didn't mind though, because she always let me buy an ice cream cone or candy bar with the change. It wasn't a long walk, maybe a mile at the most and I always took my dog with me. My walk to the store went over a canal just before reaching the highway.

On each trip to and from the store, I'd practice tightrope walking on the pipeline which spanned the canal. Falling in would mean muddy clothes and another willow switch when I got home. It became an incentive not to fall, and with each crossing, my balance improved. The possibility of one day becoming a tightrope walker with the circus was a driving force in my weekly practice. To develop the skills I needed, I thought Grandma should expect me to come home wet and muddy once in a while, but she just wasn't very understanding.

I was ready to start the dangerous walk across the pipe and hummed the sound of a trumpet out loud. Thousands of imaginary people far below watched in awe as I took the first step. Out of the corner of my eye, I saw an old beat up brown car stop on the one lane bridge. I glanced toward the car and saw two men watching me. An audience, I smiled to myself, and another reason not to fall. Maybe I should charge them to watch.

Just as I was about to take my second step, the driver yelled to me; "Hey kid, come over here."

The canal bank was covered with thorns, so I carefully picked my steps back to the bridge to see what they wanted.

"We just stopped to give you a ride. You're going to the store aren't you?" the man asked.

"Yes sir, I am, but it's not that far and I have my dog with me." I felt uneasy about the strangers. Something just wasn't right.

"Come on, just get in," the driver said as he opened his door and motioned toward the back seat. "Your dog can ride, too. I know your Grandma, and she said it's okay."

I studied their faces and could see they were serious. The man on the passenger side had a baseball cap on his head with the bill turned backwards and chewing tobacco on his lower teeth. The hair on the back of my neck stood up like red warning flags.

"No thanks, I'm just going to walk." I backed away from the car and considered running but knew they could catch me.

"Then do me a big favor," the driver said. "Would you look behind our car and see if we're dragging something?" Cautiously, I walked behind the car but kept my distance.

"No, I don't see anything," I yelled to them, my mouth almost too dry to speak. The words hadn't left my mouth before their tires were spinning, and the car was racing backwards towards Skippy and me.

I ran out of the car's path, but their back tire ran over Skippy.

They slid to a stop with me standing beside their car in a state of shock. Skippy was under the car yelping as the passenger jumped out of the car and ran towards me. The driver was opening his door so there was nowhere to go to get away from them except over the side of the bridge. There was no time to think about other options.

I looked down at the water, then back at the men and jumped over the side just before they were close enough to grab me.

It wasn't too far to the water, maybe ten feet at the most, but I shot into the water feet first and sank into the black mud up to my knees.

I looked up toward the bridge expecting the men to be standing there looking down at me, but instead I heard their doors slam, and the car roared off toward the highway.

As the dust settled, I wondered if they had taken Skippy as I could no longer hear her. When I climbed up the canal bank, I could see her lying motionless on the bridge. My eyes flooded with tears as I picked Skippy up in my arms and carried her home, crying.

Grandma was working in the garden when I walked up dripping wet, covered with mud.

"Cliff, how many times have I told you to stay off that pipe?" Grandma was already headed toward the willow tree.

"But Grandma, let me tell you what happened," I protested.

As I came closer, Grandma could see Skippy in my arms and ran to meet me.

"Cliff, what happened?" I began to tell her when she interrupted.

"Are you telling me the truth?"

"Yes Ma'am, I swear, I'm not lying. I had to jump in the water to keep them from catching me."

Grandma had a worried look on her face as she rinsed me off with the garden hose. I couldn't help wonder what she was thinking—if she had some idea who would do this and why.

After a few hours Grandma allowed me to play but insisted I stay within eyesight of our house. Finally, I talked her into letting me go to Sarah Simmons house, so she could help me bury Skippy. After all, Sarah was practically an expert at directing funerals. Each time we found a dead frog, Sarah insisted we have a proper burial so it's soul would go to Heaven.

Still shaken by the incident, I couldn't wait to tell Sarah about the men on the bridge. The two of us sat in the shade of a big oak tree in front of her house as I gave her the play-by-play details. Sarah listened intently, then ran into her house, and came out with her brother's baseball cards. One by one she had me study each card and pick out possible suspects.

"Sarah, I don't think they were baseball players. They really looked more like Elvis Presley."

"Cliff, just shut up and keep looking. There has to be someone in all these cards that looks like the bad guys that tried to kidnap you."

I looked through the stacks of baseball cards until I was sick of looking at them. When I glanced up, Sarah gave me a death glare.

"Keep looking!"

A few of them looked like tough guys but Sarah insisted I

pick two that looked like the men on the bridge. Carefully, I studied the cards again and found three who looked slightly similar.

Sarah studied my choices. "It figures," she said. They are all Yankees from up north.

She was convinced. "Those Yankees can't be trusted. They're probably somewhere in Texas playing baseball and trying to kidnap someone else right now."

I was really more concerned about the loss of Skippy than the men on the bridge. My best friend in the whole world was dead, and my heart was broken. I thought about the times Grandma made me sandwiches, and how I would take them outside and take turns sharing bites with Skippy off the same side of the bread. Grandma tried to get me to tear off pieces and feed her that way, but it was okay, I knew Skippy didn't mind eating off the same side that I did. It didn't seem to bother her at all. Everywhere we went, we had been "partners in crime" and shared the blame for damaged gardens or doo doo piles equally.

Sarah could sense my sadness and agreed to help me bury Skippy. She suggested we have a full funeral and started making plans about what friends to invite. I preferred to just keep the funeral simple, because I didn't want anyone to see me cry.

Sarah and I went back to my house and loaded Skippy in my wagon, covering her with a towel. There was a field with a slight hill not far from my house that we chose for the burial site. We really needed a monument of some kind to mark the grave. I believe Sarah was thinking along the lines of a wooden cross, but an idea hit me as hard as a hammer.

"I know—we'll get one from the Turner Cemetery."

Sarah seemed surprised, but I explained that the cemetery was started by my ancestors. So, just like the trees in Bridge City, the cemetery was really mine too. Sarah thought about it for a while, then bit her lower lip and nodded in agreement. It wasn't a bad idea. Grandma and I were related to most of the people buried there and she kept a key hanging on the kitchen wall for the cemetery gate. I knew right from wrong. I knew it was right to give Skippy a monument, but also knew it would be wrong to ask Grandma for the cemetery key because she, of course, would say no. The safest thing to do was sneak the key out when she wasn't looking.

The key was easy enough to hide, but Grandma saw I had something hidden under my shirt and asked me what I had. Embarrassed that I was caught, I pulled my shirt up and showed her the quart jar of blackberries I had taken from her pantry. Quickly, I explained that Sarah and I needed the blackberries for a picnic we were going to have after we buried Skippy. She just smiled, handed me two spoons and said be sure to bring the jar back.

The cemetery was shadowed by moss-draped live oaks, and the wind seemed to whisper in a ghostly, spiritual voice. Being sensitive to my surroundings, I felt a cold shiver run through me as Sarah and I walked silently looking at all the tombstones.

"Cliff, don't step on the graves! The ghost of the person will

haunt you!" I jumped quickly to the side and apologized to anyone listening.

We finally settled for a small stone marker near the back of
the cemetery with a faded name that neither of us could read.
It was a lot of work to dig it up and was even harder to load it
in the wagon, but we were determined. The wagon turned over
a few times as we pulled and pushed our heavy load out the
front gate and across Morning Glory Drive into the field.

Sarah and I took turns digging and then placed Skippy in the
dark soil at the bottom of the hole. Carefully, we wrestled the
stone monument in the ground over Skippy and packed the
extra dirt around the sides. We held hands as we both said
prayers and spoke about what a great dog she had been.

"Maybe God needed a fishing partner," Sarah whispered softly as she gave me a hug and brushed a tear off my dirt covered
cheek.

"Yea or maybe the angels in Heaven needed a good watch
dog to guard the gate," I added.

In bright red crayon, Sarah wrote Skippy on the monument.
She was placed in God's hands to live forever in Dog Heaven.

*NOTE: I'm sure my distant relatives were in shock to find
their loved one's headstone missing the next time they visited the
cemetery. I offer you my deepest apologies for any pain this may
have caused you. I know it was a horrible thing to do, but the
truth is, the person buried there probably looked down from
heaven that day and smiled.*

The whole thing with the men on the bridge and Skippy getting killed was haunting me. Who were the men and what did

they want? Were they really trying to kidnap me or were they just playing around? What would have happened if I hadn't jumped in the canal? What if I had gotten in the car with them? I wondered if Uncle Rudy had hired some of his friends to kill me. Maybe one of the men was my dad and he just wanted to meet me. Perhaps give me a ride so he could learn more about me.

That night I had another bad dream. It wasn't about the men on the bridge or Skippy, but Uncle Rudy again. He was chasing me down the road in a car. Just before he was close enough to run over me, I dove into a culvert that ran under the road near our house.

Uncle Rudy drove off into the ditch and continuously rammed into the end of the culvert causing more and more of the crumbling concrete to break off. With each collision, I would back further away from the end until there was very little of the culvert left. The air was full of dust, and I was struggling to breathe.

My own whimpering must have awakened me and I moved to the security of Grandma's room, curling up with a blanket on her floor.

A culvert did pass under the road near our house. It must have entered my dream because Sarah's brother, Ray, told me trolls lived there. Any time I walked over the culvert I would keep my eyes peeled to make sure nothing jumped out to get me. If it was dark and I was walking home from a friend's house, I would beg them to walk me as far as the culvert, and then watch as I ran across. Strangely enough after the dream, I was no longer frightened of the culvert and even started playing inside it. I considered it a safe place where I could hide if necessary—a concrete barrier from the dangers of my world.

CHAPTER
EIGHT

I t had been five months since Uncle Rudy had left, and any day his ship would return. Grandma wanted to believe he would be able to avoid the temptation of all the bars in Port Arthur. She knew all too well that his crew would make a mad dash to make up for lost time, and most likely Uncle Rudy would be right there with them. Even if he made it past the barrage of bars in Port Arthur without stopping, the highway came right past the Sparkle Club at the edge of Bridge City and that was his favorite.

Though Uncle Rudy had told Grandma he was sorry for what he had done to me, she worried about him coming home drunk again. If he was sober everything would be fine, but his drinking was unpredictable. Now with Verna living with us the danger of his temper exploding in a violent rage was even greater. After all, look what happened the last time he was home, and now there was a third mouth his money was helping to feed.

I still worried about Mr. Trahan talking to Uncle Rudy about his missing tree. What if Mr. Simmons told Uncle Rudy I showed up at his house naked and covered with mud, or smeared catsup on his door? Then there was the missing monument from the Turner Cemetery that was yet to be discovered. With my luck the tombstone probably belonged to one of Uncle Rudy's favorite relatives. He would probably just kill me on the spot if he found out. For a boy in the first grade, I sure had a lot of things to worry about.

After a lot of soul searching, Grandma decided it would be best if she could find another place for Verna and me to live. I cried as she explained that as much as she loved us, she was very worried. She spent a lot of time on her knees praying and waiting for God to give her an answer.

Grandma said she had written my Mom and explained the situation with Uncle Rudy, and asked if there was someway she could come and get me. It had been almost a month since she had mailed the letter and she still hadn't received an answer.

Of course I was a little worried about living with someone that I didn't even know, but thought it may be nice to have a mom. I grew tired of other kids asking me why I lived with my Grandma instead of my Mom and Dad.

Grandma thought if Verna wrote her dad and apologized for running away, he would send her the money for a bus ticket and allow her to return home. After all, he had always forgiven her before.

"If my Mom doesn't let me live with her, can I go with Verna?" I asked, hoping one of them would say yes. I noticed Verna looked sad, so I turned toward Grandma for an answer.

"No you can't, Cliff. You just don't understand."

I wanted to understand, but nobody would tell me. Crying, I ran out the back door and down the road to my security culvert. I noticed Verna following as I crawled inside. To my surprise, she crawled in with me. In a soft voice she asked if we could talk. I was glad that the darkness of the culvert helped to hide my tears, but I listened as she spoke.

"Cliff, do you know what abortion means?"

"No," I answered puzzled.

"It means stopping a pregnancy before a baby is born."

"Ok, but what does that have to do with anything," I asked still confused.

"That's what my Dad wanted your mom to do before you were born. He wanted her to have an abortion, and that's part of why you can't go to Houston with me."

"So what would happen to me if my Mom had an abortion?" I asked, almost sure what her answer would be but not wanting to believe it.

"You would be dead. That's why she ran away when she was 15, because she didn't want that to happen to you. Don't you understand?"

"Yea, I understand everyone wants me dead! The only thing I don't understand is why everyone hates me so much."

"No one wants you dead and no one hates you, Cliff. Your grandpa just thought your mom was too young to have a baby, that's all. He doesn't hate you."

"Well I know Uncle Rudy hates me, and what about the men on the bridge that tried to kill me?"

"I don't know Cliff. It just isn't a good idea for you to go to Houston with me. Besides, your Grandpa will be working all day and there won't be anyone to watch you."

"Why can't you," I asked?"

"Because I'll have to find a job—that is if he even lets me come back, or I may go back to school. My dad is very stubborn, and even though he's your grandpa, I don't think he would let you live with us."

"See, I told you he hates me. He probably paid Uncle Rudy to kill me and when that didn't work, he hired those men on the bridge."

Verna could see that discussing this was going no where. As we lay in the culvert face to face, Verna told me things that had always been off limits with Grandma. I learned that my Mom worked at a carnival with her husband Morris. Verna explained that their job required traveling from city to city, and they had asked Grandma to let me stay with her because it was just too hard to take care of me with that lifestyle. Verna explained that I had two younger brothers. One named Rocky and another named Donnie that had died when he was about six months old. She went on to say that my Mom had another baby a few years after I was born that she gave up for adoption in Orange, Texas but she didn't know if it was a boy or a girl.

I asked Verna questions about Donnie but she didn't know much. He was born in Big Springs, Texas and died in Pasadena, Texas. When I asked about Rocky, Verna said that he was about three years older than Donnie.

"So why did my Mom keep Rocky and Donnie, but left me with Grandma?"

The question burned in my heart like a hot knife, and seemed to echo in the culvert. Verna started to answer but the words caught in her throat.

"Why didn't she give me up for adoption too?"

"I'm not sure," Verna answered, knowing that my feelings were hurt.

Though painful, I grabbed at the chance for more information as Verna continued to answer questions I could never ask anyone before.

"What do you know about my Dad?" I asked hoping she had answers to the list of questions growing in my mind.

"I know he plays guitar in a Cajun band, and I believe your mom said he lives in Port Arthur, but I don't know much more about him."

"Do you know what his name is?" I asked.

"I've heard it a few times, but I just don't remember. It's a Cajun name, not Johnson like your last name. I know he came to see what you looked like when you were a baby and your grandpa fired a gun at him. I think he was afraid to come back after that."

"So why is my last name Johnson?" I asked; both puzzled and surprised at what she had told me.

Verna's eyes grew misty as I waited for her answer.

"I'm really not sure, Cliff. Maybe your mom met some guy after she ran away and just blamed the pregnancy on him. It could be she married someone named Johnson. I just don't have all the answers."

The concrete culvert felt cold against my bare stomach as Verna and I lay there in the shadows facing each other. Her eyes looked like mirrors reflecting my own blurred tears. After she ran out of answers, I agreed to go back to our house.

As we walked holding hands, Verna made me promise not to discuss what we had talked about with anyone else. For some reason I felt comforted having the answers to a few of my questions, though I was hurt by some of the truths.

CHAPTER

NINE

Saturday morning arrived with a slight hint of winter in southeast Texas. After a breakfast of blackberry cobbler, I sat down on the couch and turned on the radio. Searching the dial, I settled on the Lone Ranger, demonstrating the difference between good and evil. Yelling out his famous "Hi-Yo, Silver, away!" as the orchestra played the William Tell Overture in the background.

Growing impatient with my morning radio show, Verna walked in from the kitchen and changed the dial to a music station. Verna glanced out the window and let out a gasp, followed by; "Oh my God!" Her face turned pale. Jumping up, I rushed to the window to see what she was gawking at.

An old rusty pickup truck was parked in the driveway with the hood up, allowing a cloud of steam to rise in the cool morning air. A short stocky man about fifty years old faded in and out of view in the mist as he looked down at the motor. A large lady about the same age as the man climbed out and staggered toward our house, frowning at the man as she passed.

Verna let out another long; "Oh—my—God!"

"Who is that?" I asked, confused by Verna's reaction.

"Momma," Verna sighed, as if her visit wasn't a good thing.

"My Mom," I asked, thinking that she didn't look at all like the pictures I had seen.

"No, not your mom Cliff, it's mine. I haven't seen her in years," Verna whispered.

I glanced toward Grandma and noticed she was crying, but I couldn't tell if she was happy or sad. I wanted to ask her what was wrong, but there wasn't time; the lady was opening our front door.

Verna's mom stood a full 6' tall, with dark hair streaked with gray and a dark complexion. Her face looked hard and leathery as she puffed on a cigarette. Her red finger nails drew my attention and I noticed they were missing polish in a few places. Her husband came in right behind her. About 5'3" tall, his face appeared pitted with small pock marks.

After an exchange of hugs, Grandma laughed and said; "Cliff thought you were his mom." That brought laughs from everyone, but I didn't see anything funny about it.

"Well son, your mom would be really upset if she comes back and hears you calling me *mom*. Grandma makes me feel too damn old. Why don't you just call me Big Mama?"

"Okay," I answered bashfully.

"This is my husband Pat, but you can call him Papaw. I understand you need a place to live?"

"Yes Ma'am," I answered, still embarrassed by her directness.

"Well for some reason your mom can't take care of you, so I guess that makes you my responsibility. Not that I'm complaining. If your going to live with us you may as well know right now that we're not uppity people."

Not knowing what to say, I looked at Grandma for a sign of approval. She didn't offer any hint if I should go or not, so it was settled just like that. I had a new place to live.

Big Mama gave Verna a hard look, and slowly shook her head from side to side as if she was disgusted.

"What are you doing here?" Big Mama asked in a hateful voice.

"Just visiting," Verna replied with a hint of sarcasm as she whirled and walked out the door.

I had been around Verna long enough to know that something was wrong. It was easy to see the tension between her and Big Mama. I wanted to follow her and find out what was wrong, but thought I better wait.

"I was going to offer Verna a place to live too. Now little Miss Goody-Two-Shoes can just stay in Houston with her worthless dad for all I care," Big Mama spouted.

"Get your things packed son," Big Mama said.

"Papaw wants to go by the lumber yard and buy some material to make you a bed. He plans to get you a mattress from the Navy base next week, so you'll just have to get by with a blanket for now."

"Can I go tell my friends goodbye? It will only take a few minutes," I begged.

"I need to check some of the bars and see if I can find a job. We'll pick you up in two hours. That'll give you plenty of time to tell your friends bye and pack your things. We just moved to Orange, so it's not like you're going to be that far away."

Verna was in the shade of the trees behind our house, staring at a group of minnows in the ditch when I walked up beside her.

"What you looking at?" I asked, not knowing if she wanted my company.

"Have you ever noticed how the minnows all move together in unison, like they know what each others thoughts are? It doesn't matter how clouded the water is, they all turn at the same time, yet stay at each others side. They're like a big happy family that can't be split up."

"Yea they can, watch this!" I yelled, as I bombarded the minnows with dirt clods, sending them scrambling in all directions.

"See? I told you!"

Verna started sobbing and wiped her tears off her cheeks with her fingers.

"You just don't understand, Cliff. Our family is as dysfunctional as they come. We're not like other families. Doesn't that bother you?"

"Do you want to go to the culvert and talk?" I asked, ignoring her question.

"No, you're getting big enough that you can talk without having to hide in the shadows. Let's walk to the cemetery."

"Shouldn't we get the key," I asked?

"No, I don't want to go back in the house. We can climb over the gate."

"So what's wrong?" I asked, after we had walked halfway to the cemetery in silence.

"It's just everything. You're going to be living in the same environment that I grew up hating. It's like a continuing cycle with no way out."

"So do you think—I shouldn't live with Big Mama," I asked?

"Well it doesn't look like you have a choice. My Mom is an alcoholic and I'm guessing her husband is too. At least you won't have to worry about Uncle Rudy and what he might do if given the opportunity. Bridge City is close enough that you can still see Grandma and your friends occasionally."

"Is Big Mama mean?" I asked, hoping Verna's answer would be no.

"She can be, but I don't think she'll be mean to you. If you were a girl that wanted to dress nice or wear makeup, it would be different. But you like to hunt and fish, so I'm sure you'll fit in better than I did."

"How was Big Mama mean?" I asked. That part was still brothering me.

"Oh it's just things that she's done. Her I *don't take crap from anyone attitude* caused her quite a few problems. Like the time the man from Gulf States Utilities Company came to shut off our electricity and she fired a warning shot into the pole above his head."

"Wow, did she plan to shoot him and miss?" I asked.

"I don't know. He slid back down the pole and the power stayed on for a few more hours—at least until he came back with the sheriff. Big Mama served some time in the woman's prison in Huntsville, but that's something else that no one talks about. It was just another dark secret to mold and mildew with the other skeletons in our family closet."

"Your mom was in prison! Who took care of you?"

"Daddy did most of the time. They were already divorced when she went to prison."

Verna and I walked through the cemetery looking at the gravestones as we talked. I reminded her about the "don't step of the graves rule" I had recently learned.

"See that headstone? Ben Turner is your great-great grandfather. He was in the Texas Cavalry and born in 1843, and that one over there is Everett Johnston, your great grandfather. Did you know that Jon Turner was one of the guys that signed the Texas Declaration of Independence when the battle of the Alamo was being fought? He was your great-great-great grandfather."

"Do you think he knew Davy Crockett or Jim Bowie?" I asked.

"I don't know, but our ancestors all played such an important role in history. It's a shame to have their descendants turn out like they did," Verna answered as she stared at the inscription.

I considered what Verna was saying, but we didn't seem all that bad to me. We go to church at least twice a week.

"I want to be buried right there when I die," Verna said pointing at a spot in the shadows. "Listen to the wind. Doesn't it sound peaceful?"

"No, it sounds spooky to me," I said, glancing at the small hole where a missing gravestone had been and hoping Verna didn't notice it.

We climbed back over the cemetery gate and started walking back toward the house. I could tell that Verna was still in deep thought.

"So why did Big Mama and your dad divorce," I asked?

"Grandpa came in late from work one night, drunk as usual. He started complaining about what Mama was cooking for supper and the way she kept the house. Of course Mama wasn't happy about him drinking without her and his complaining didn't help matters. He had just sat down at the table and made a comment about how the chicken looked like burnt crow. With no warning, Mama hit him over the head with a full skillet of scalding hot gravy."

"I bet he was really mad," I laughed.

"Mad? You don't even know what the word means! Your Grandpa sat there stunned as the hot gravy ran down his head and dripped onto his shoulders. His balding head was badly burned, but Mama didn't offer him any sympathy. His temper exploded! He wanted to hit her, but Mama stood her ground ready to hit him again if he tried. They divorced just a short time after that."

Verna decided she didn't want to come in the house, and was going to visit Aunt Lilly. She didn't want to be home when Big Mama returned, so we said our goodbyes.

"You're a tough little boy. Everything will be fine," Verna reassured me.

CHAPTER
TEN

Everything I owned fit in two cardboard boxes, except for my wagon. It was just a short drive to where we would be living.

When we pulled up in front of their home I was in disbelief. The house was huge. It set on the corner across the street from the Trailways Bus Station. It looked almost like an old mansion from a horror movie.

"Holy cow! This is your house?" I asked

"No, this is our rat hole apartment," Big Mama answered, her voice full of sarcasm. She must have seen the puzzled look on my face.

"You think I'm kidding? Well just wait and you'll see what I mean. There are rats as big as dogs outside our window each morning. The first damn time I see one in the apartment, we're moving out of this shit hole." Papaw cautioned her on her language, but Big Mama snapped back. "By God if he's going to live with us, then he just as well learn how we are. If he doesn't like it, then he can always go back to his grandma's."

I quickly settled into life in the city, but I sure missed the freedom I had in Bridge City. Big Mama was right about the rats. Each morning we would watch them running around the trash piled outside the apartment. Big Mama would go into a cussing rage; "Someone should burn this place down. The damn wall paper is falling off the wall, the paint is cracked and peeling, and water keeps dripping from the bathroom upstairs. We're not going to live here another damn month if I have anything to say about it."

Papaw finished building my bed, and added blankets with U.S. Navy printed on them. Each day he would come home from the navy base and empty his duffel bag on the table. It was almost as good as Christmas. He kept us supplied with a steady flow of meat and canned goods, all compliments of the government. Even our silverware and dishes had U.S. Navy printed on them. You might say Papaw took full advantage of all his government benefits.

Big Mama found a job working as a barmaid in Orange where a lot of the Navy men and shipyard workers hung out. Papaw didn't seem to care for the idea of her working there.

"It just isn't very lady like," Papaw would say.

Going to the bar was a new experience for me. Dark, mysterious and smoke-filled, it possessed a certain glamour that could only be experienced through the eyes of a young boy. The deep bass sounds from the Wurlitzer Jukebox pumped out country songs so loud the beer mugs would vibrate on the tables. Its glowing neon columns produced a rainbow of dazzling colors. Bubbles percolated up the sides of the jukebox, producing a hypnotic effect as I watched with glazed eyes.

A shuffleboard table lined one wall and I would spend hours sliding the pucks back and forth begging for someone to play the game with me. Once in awhile I found a taker, but most of the time I was on my own.

I was curious about the Navy men and shipyard workers but sometimes frightened by the rowdiness. The bar had a hole-in-the-wall atmosphere, but only small quantities of rowdiness were tolerated. Otherwise Big Mama would step in. She was big enough that she probably didn't need the pool cue she carried in the ready position, drawn back, waiting to be released on anyone who gave her back talk.

"I'll make a believer out of you! I'm going to turn this into a respectable establishment come hell or high water," she would yell. It sure got my attention, and there was no doubt in my mind that she would smack someone in the head if she needed to.

Some of the clientele didn't want a respectable establishment and complained to the bar owner. When he talked to Big Mama about her temperament, she told him he could just go to hell and stormed out the door with me in tow.

⟢⟑⟣

Papaw decided to retire, so with Big Mama not working, it just gave them more time together. He had served his country faithfully for twenty years. During that time he had seven ships blown out from under him and had been held as a prisoner, eventually escaping from a Japanese prison camp. He wasn't one to brag, but the shrapnel Big Mama dug out of the wounds on his back, told me he had experienced war at its worst. I would cringe as Big Mama squeezed small pieces of metal shrapnel out of his skin, and placed them on a napkin with the tweezers.

I think Papaw drank to block out the horrors he experienced during the war, but he always seemed to be a humorous, caring man. With no kids of his own he took a genuine interest in me. Fighting and survival skills were at the top of the list of things he thought I should learn. He devoted a lot of time teaching me to hunt and fish, but how to kill a man with a bayonet or strangle a person to death was probably not something I needed in elementary school. I'm sure these were just things he knew well and thought he needed to share with me. Maybe that was all he knew how to give.

Purposely, Papaw would capsize a small rowboat, *he found* somewhere, and then teach me how to use the rivers current to our advantage to make it to shore. Sometimes when he turned the boat upside down, we would stick our heads up into the air pocket underneath as the boat drifted downstream. He was so confident in his training that I was seldom in fear.

On weekends, Papaw proudly took me on tours of the navy base, pointing out each ship's characteristics. Being a strong patriotic man and Navy most of his life, he was convinced I would follow in his footsteps. I too, envisioned someday becoming a Navy Seal specializing in underwater demolition.

❦

We woke up one morning to find water running out of the ceiling above us. Even with the buckets Big Mama placed under the cascading water, everything in our apartment was getting soaked. Big Mama tried contacting the landlord, and when that didn't work the police were called. They had to break into the apartment above us. The guy living there was drunk and passed out in the bathtub with the water turned on full force.

Big Mama was in a rage and insisted she needed whiskey to calm her nerves. It seemed like the more she drank, the angrier she became. When the landlord did arrive, Big Mama was primed and ready to argue. She started with all the problems the apartment had, and then covered the rats and high rent.

The landlord didn't seem to be too concerned, and that just made her madder. Papaw finally just told her to shut the hell up.

"I swear to God, I'll burn this rat hole down!" she exploded.

"Damn it, just calm down! Your going to get us kicked out before we find another place to live!" Papaw yelled as he pulled Big Mama back to our apartment by the arm.

"I promise I'll find a better place. You just need to have a little patience," Papaw pleaded.

With Papaw retired and Big Mama not working, they decided there was no reason to live in town. Each day we went on drives, searching for a place in the country, but only found new bars they wanted to check out.

One afternoon Papaw came home with the exciting news. He had found the perfect place, and best of all, it was near Bridge City.

We moved to a house just a few miles out of Bridge City right on the shore of Sabine Lake. I thought I had died and went to heaven. The house wasn't much to look at. Just a shack by any standards, but that part didn't matter to me. The important thing was its location. It was close enough to Bridge City that I could walk to Grandma's if I wanted.

About a mile and a half of the road was covered with oyster shells that had been pounded into a fine white powder by the many vehicles that had used the road over the years. A canal followed one side of the road with no bank or guard rails, while the other side of road was marsh land as far as the eye could see. The road had once been the route to the Dryden Ferry dock where travelers would cross the Neches River to the refineries and businesses in Port Arthur.

Big Mama would grab the dash and yell at Papaw to slow down as he dodged the water holes which covered the road as we bounced along in our old truck. Once in a while he would purposely hit one, causing water to spray the windshield. I would laugh and Big Mama would cuss and grab the dash in fear. She was terrified he would lose control and slide off into the canal.

"Damn it! The alligators will eat us before we can get out of the water, if we don't drown. Now quit playing around!" she yelled.

For a moment I considered her comment and then smiled. I knew Papaw drove well enough that he wouldn't run off into the canal. Besides, I had never seen an alligator in this canal.

On weekends at almost every pullout along the road, families could be seen crabbing. Of course anyone I saw on what I considered our property received an evil eye. I felt like everything within a mile of our house was my exclusive territory, and they were trespassing in "Cliff's Kingdom." The marsh land, the bayou and even that part of Sabine Lake were all part of my empire. Of course I couldn't tell anyone that, but it didn't stop me from giving them a mean look.

Bailey's Fish Camp/Dance Hall was next door to our house and Sabine Lake was just across the road. When the wind was from the right direction I could almost smell the cotton candy at Pleasure Island, an amusement park across the lake near Port Arthur.

Fishermen would often stop by Bailey's on the way home to show off their catch. I would stand with my mouth open and marvel at the size of some of their fish. I learned if I had my fishing pole with me and acted interested enough, they would usually give me a nice size fish. I was learning to be a professional con man and would always bring home *"my catch"* with a big grin on my face. Big Mama and Papaw always acted so proud of me that I couldn't tell them I didn't catch it myself. Thinking back, they probably knew the truth and just went along with my act.

The air at Bailey's was always filled with the smell of crab boil or gumbo. More importantly, Grandma Bailey was always willing to feed me if I just happened to stop by at the right time. She wasn't my Grandma, but that's what everyone called her. Besides, it never hurts to have an extra Grandma – especially one who's a good cook.

Bailey's was a huge two story wooden structure with faded paint on the outside, the results of the pounding it took from the violent storms that blew in across Sabine Lake from the Gulf of Mexico. An old rusted tin roof covered the top and made a tranquil, hypnotic sound when the rain came pouring down.

The second floor of Bailey's was the dance hall. A dance hall in the marsh seemed almost out of place. Its wooden floor was polished to a high gloss, reflecting the light which flooded in. The second floor windows offered a beautiful view of the surrounding marsh land and the magnificent Rainbow Bridge could be seen in the distance.

I would often go upstairs by myself and sing, pretending there was a crowd dancing or that I was entertaining at the Grand Ole Opry in Nashville. The large empty room had an echo, kind of like singing into an old oil barrel. I would belt out "You Ain't Nothing But A Hound Dog" and "Blueberry Hill" or some of the other popular songs I had learned at the bar in Orange.

A lot of weekends, Big Mama would drop me off at Grandma's while they went out drinking. I didn't mind bouncing back and forth because that gave me a chance to play with my friends.

Living with Big Mama and Papaw was a big change from staying at Grandma's. Grandma took me to church at every opportunity and had me memorizing Bible verses. It was almost like being raised in an environment of good, versus evil; there was spiritual warfare taking place before my very eyes and I was being pulled both ways.

At Big Mama's I learned to cuss like a sailor, play poker, shoot dice and could fart in the kitchen if I felt the need. Try that at Grandma's and I'd get a willow switch across my butt. A few times I considered not playing for a few hours, and breaking all the willow switches that were close enough to the ground for Grandma to reach off the tree. You might say it was my own form of homeland security.

Each time Big Mama and Papaw had me bring them a beer out of the refrigerator I was allowed to have a sip. At my age it didn't take too many drinks to feel the effects of the alcohol. There was Jax, Lone Star, Pearl, Miller and my favorite, Falstaff. The thing I liked most about staying there was they often allowed me to skip school. Heck, the way I saw it, I had already learned how to add and subtract playing cards. I learned to read by studying the labels on beer cans so what did I need school for anyway?

What a place to grow up! A huge lake with ships, tug boats, a canal just three hundred feet away and the Old River Bayou within a quarter of a mile. The broad expanse of a coastal marsh stretched for miles behind our house, inviting me to explore. Fishing, crabbing, shrimp, and oh yes, I almost forgot the ever-present danger of an occasional alligator just to keep me alert.

This area of Sabine Lake probably wasn't the best place to swim, but I did it anyway. Rusty nails and spikes from the Old Dryden Ferry dock littered the bottom and an occasional oil or gas slick with beautiful rainbow colors floated on the waters surface. Little things like that didn't stop me from swimming.

Occasionally, I would see a Texaco ship turn in the channel on Sabine Lake and head up the Neches River toward the refineries. Each time I fought off the chill that ran up my back and wondered if Uncle Rudy was on board.

One afternoon a shiny black car with out of state license plates drove by and the man driving eyed me as he passed. He looked kind of suspicious, so I stood there in the waist deep water with my hands on my hips and returned my "you're trespassing" stare back at him. Probably one of them damn Yankees from up north, I thought to myself. I wasn't sure exactly what a Yankee was, but that's what Big Mama said each time she saw an out of state license plate. Big Mama considered anywhere north of Texas to be Yankee country.

The man stopped a short distance up the road near the bridge where the Old River Bayou emptied into Sabine Lake and took out a fishing pole. He had only been fishing a short time when I heard yelling as he ran toward his car waving his arms. Laughing to myself, I wondered if he got to close to the wasp nest I had seen under the bridge.

"That should teach that city slicker Yankee not to come down here again," I laughed.

The man slammed his car door shut and the rear end of his car slid around fishtailing as he raced toward me. The car was kicking up a cloud of dirt, and I stood up in the water to watch him roar past. Big Mama wasn't going to like the way he was driving. She had just hung her wash out on the clothes line to dry. If they got covered with dust she was going to be really mad. When the car got even to where I was standing, it slid to a halt, and the man jumped out in the cloud of dust.

"You better hurry and get out of that water," he yelled. "There's some kind of monster over there," he said, pointing toward where he had been fishing. I stood there with water up to my chest, thinking he was joking until he repeated it again.

"Didn't you hear what I said? Get out of that water!"

He was so excited, jumping up and down and waving his arms that I thought maybe I better do what he said. When I reached shore he jumped in his car and sped off, leaving me and our clothesline in his cloud of dust.

Big Mama and Papaw came running out of the house to see what all the commotion was about just as the car slid around the corner by Bailey's headed for Bridge City, full speed. Big Mama was cussing toward the cloud of dust and shaking her fist, but there was no way he could have heard what she was yelling.

Papaw came out behind Big Mama and I told them what the man had said about the monster. He decided we would walk down to the bridge and check it out. I pointed out where the man had been fishing and Papaw spotted a very expensive rod and reel lying on the ground where the man had been standing. The fishing line still led into the water so Papaw started reeling in the line until it went taut.

"It must have hung up on the old bridge pilings," Papaw said.

He walked waist deep into the murky water, tugging on the fishing line and reeling in the slack. Papaw thought he had broken the line, when it went slack, but then it started moving into deeper water.

"It doesn't feel like a gar. It must be a red or a flounder, and I can tell it's going to be a big one. I just hope I can play it in without breaking the line!" Papaw yelled excitedly.

Papaw took his time and seemed to be gaining on his fight with the monster as I stood close, ready to help pull it in.

When the line stretched almost straight down in the water below us, the monster broke the surface and our mystery was over. A huge alligator did a death roll on the end of the line as I ran for shore. Taking out his knife, Papaw cut the line and let the alligator go.

I guess the man didn't know that we have alligators in Texas. We laughed about that for a long time and Papaw acquired an expensive rod and reel.

Chapter TWELVE

I was at Grandma's when a taxi pulled up in our driveway. It's probably Uncle Rudy I thought, feeling a frown tighten my face. I really hoped it was someone else. Guess I'll be staying at Big Mama's while he's home, I thought.

"For heaven sake, it's your mom!" Grandma yelled as she headed out the door to greet her.

My Mom! I stood there in shock letting the words register.

I followed Grandma outside, but I wasn't sure how to act. Mom came up to me with a big smile on her face and her arms open, expecting a hug. She was dressed nicer than anyone I had ever seen in Bridge City, except maybe Verna. Her perfume smelled like some of the women who went to our church, only it seemed a lot stronger. I was really shy and bashful around her, but I was also curious to know more about her and craved the attention she was showing me.

"Did you miss me?" she asked with a beaming smile.

I could feel my face burning from embarrassment. What did she expect me to say?

Yes Ma'am," I answered, with my eyes turned toward the floor.

The truth was, I hadn't really missed her at all, but then I really didn't know her either. It seemed kind of strange to be giving her the hugs she asked for. Mom had a little boy with her and she introduced him as my brother Rocky. Mom said he was named Rocky after the famous fighter Rocky Marciano. She said they were living in Downey, California, and wanted me to come live with them.

Mom seemed so excited that it was hard to say no, but how could I just take off with someone I didn't even know? Mom said that Verna could go too, and seeing Verna's excitement helped to convince me that maybe the move might be a good thing.

"What about all my friends?" I thought to myself. I don't want to leave them behind.

"Will we ever be coming back?" I asked my Mom, still unsure. After all, Big Mama, Papaw and Grandma would all miss me.

"Maybe someday, but not for a very long time," Mom answered.

Mom must have seen the worried look on my face because she pulled me close and gave me another big hug. I hugged her back, but it felt so strange. Even Grandma and Verna didn't hug me that tight, and it felt uncomfortable.

"Won't it be great for us all to be a family again?

"Yes Ma'am," I answered, trying to show as much enthusiasm as she had shown.

"Morris will be so glad to see you after all these years." Mom's face was aglow.

"Who is Morris," I asked, knowing that name seemed familiar, and then remembering Verna had told me he is married to my Mom.

"He's your dad. Well really your step-dad but I guess you were too young to remember him."

I wondered if I should have agreed to go with Mom without checking with Grandma first. What about Big Mama and Papaw? What would they think about me abandoning them? Glancing toward Grandma, I looked for her smile of approval, but it wasn't there. I felt so bad.

Verna still seemed excited about going. Why hadn't I taken more time before telling Mom I would move away with her? Grandma had raised me most of my life, and I was leaving with no notice and acting happy about it. I wasn't dissatisfied with my current life, but I didn't see any way to get out of it. Life was really starting to become very complicated, and I wasn't sure whether I had a choice in the matter.

"Cliff, have you ever heard of Disneyland?" Mom asked with her eyes wide with excitement?

"No," I answered.

"Well Disneyland is an amusement park that's ten times better than Pleasure Pier in Port Arthur," she said with an ecstatic look on her face.

"And they don't have mosquitoes," she laughed, as she slapped her arm. No mosquitoes, how would that be I wondered? My mind drifted as I thought of all the rides Disneyland must have. Yes, moving to California was going to be fun.

Since Mom had come to Bridge City on a bus, she thought it would be better to buy a car for the trip back to California. She picked out the nicest car on the sales lot. A beautiful blue 1954 Pontiac Chieftain with fender skirts and a windshield visor. Mom wrote the salesman a check like money was no object.

"Wow, she's rich," I thought to myself.

"Can we drive around town a few times so my friends can see me in this fancy car?" I asked with a grin. I felt very important as Mom beeped the horn as we drove past my friends and I waved as they stood with their mouths open. If Sarah saw me, she would probably wonder if I was kidnapped. Unfortunately, she wasn't home.

After a quick shopping trip in Beaumont, we went out to Sabine Lake and told Big Mama and Papaw goodbye. Grandma cried when we stopped in Bridge City as Verna loaded her things. After a lot of hugs, kisses, and tears we were on the way to California.

CHAPTER

THIRTEEN

At the rate we were going, I thought we would never get to California. Mom sure liked to shop and that was a new experience for me. I had never had so many new clothes and toys in all my life. If I saw something I liked at a gift shop along the way it was mine. I didn't even have to ask for it. I had started a small rock collection back in Bridge City. It was nothing fancy, just some pretty rocks I had picked up here and there. At each Indian Trading Post we stopped at, they had the most beautiful polished rocks and arrowheads I'd ever seen. Quickly I added to my collection.

After a few days of traveling we were crossing the Painted Desert on Route 66. My world had gone from subtropical green in Bridge City to multi-colored browns, blue, gray, and lavender layered flat-topped mesas and buttes. I just couldn't soak it in enough as I watched the horizon stretching into the distance. I kept my face glued to the window all the time. Rocky must have seen it all before, because he slept most of the way. Even when he was awake, he didn't seem that interested in our surroundings. For me, the highway offered a journey into the unknown and was such a change from marsh lands and bayous of east Texas.

We stopped at the Petrified Forest in Arizona and walked around as Mom took photos. I spotted a beautiful petrified stone log fragment just begging me to pick it up. A sign where we parked clearly said not to take samples, but Mom looked around and said I could take it if I hurried before anyone else pulled up. Carefully looking around, I hid the specimen in my shirt and rushed back to the car with guilt written all over my face. When Verna climbed back in the car she had three pieces that were even larger than mine. With a big smile, she gave me her specimens to add to my collection.

As we passed a motel near Holbrook, Arizona, I noticed all the rooms looked like Indian Teepees. I asked if we could stop there and spend the night, and just like magic we turned around and went back to the motel. It was like POOF! All at once I had been placed with a rich family and could have anything I wanted. I was starting to like my new lifestyle.

Shortly after we entered California, Mom had to stop at a fruit inspection station. The officer walked up to our car with his clipboard in hand, and asked Mom to open her trunk. She was shaking like a leaf in a wind storm as she got out of the car.

Instantly, I remembered my stash of petrified wood. That had to be why Mom was acting so strange. Someone must have seen us take the petrified wood and reported us. That explained why the man wanted Mom to open the trunk.

"We're all going to jail if he finds my petrified wood," I thought.

Looking Mom up and down, the officer asked her why she was so nervous.

"You would be nervous too if you had traveled as many miles as I have with these young rambunctious boys," she answered with a fake smile.

I think he looked through our car more than he normally would, but he didn't find anything illegal and didn't look twice at my petrified wood. He let us go, but kept watching us the whole time as Mom put the car in gear and drove off. Mom kept looking back in her rear-view mirror, almost like she expected him to jump in his car at any time and chase us down.

"Maybe he thinks Verna is Marilyn Monroe," I said, attempting to break the tension that filled the car. Nobody laughed. I sensed something was terribly wrong.

When we arrived in Downey, California, Mom said that Morris was going to really be excited to see me.

"He hasn't seen you since you were about two years old," Mom said with a smile.

Mom pulled the car into a parking space in front of an apartment complex and woke up Verna and Rocky.

"We're home," she announced with a tired look on her face.

Looking around at my surroundings, I was a little disappointed. California wasn't exactly what I expected. To make matters worse, I wasn't allowed to even leave the parking lot. For a boy who previously had miles to explore, this was going to be hard to accept.

I expected Morris to have the same bubbly personality that Mom had when she arrived in Bridge City, but that thought changed when we walked in the door. Morris didn't seem at all happy to see me and the expression on his face quickly changed to anger when he learned that Mom had bought a car.

"You wrote another hot check! What the hell are you thinking?" he screamed.

Mom started crying and I wondered what he meant by hot.

"The Feds won't be far behind you! We have to get rid of this car and, by God, I mean now. Sometimes you have shit for brains!" Morris yelled.

After a lot more arguing, they decided to abandon the car in a supermarket parking lot a few miles away. Carefully, Morris wiped their fingerprints off the steering wheel, dash and door handle. *What about my fingerprints on the back window,* I wondered, but was afraid to ask.

Morris drove by the supermarket a few days later and the car was gone. Over the next week, the car was about the only conversation between Mom and Morris and it always turned into another argument.

Morris's brother, Mel, was living with us in the same apartment. He was a lot more laid back and easier going than Morris. Both Verna and I became attached to him.

෨෴෨

Agents from the Federal Bureau of Investigation knocked on our apartment door just a few weeks after we arrived in California. They had a search warrant for the apartment and an arrest warrant for Mom. One of the FBI agents said Mom would be extradited to Kansas to stand trial for interstate flight to avoid prosecution.

They searched our apartment and found the check book she had used to pay for the car in Texas. I wondered if they knew she had used checks to pay for all our meals and motels during the trip to California. My knees shook as the FBI agents looked through our things. I worried they would see my petrified wood collection and arrest me, too. After all, the sign said taking samples is a federal offense.

I heard the FBI Agents tell Morris that when Kansas got through with her, Texas and a few other states would probably want her, too. The agents said Mom had been passing closed account checks all over the country. Mom was crying like I'd never seen anyone cry before. Her whole body was trembling. The agents allowed her to hug and kiss us goodbye before they handcuffed and took her away. It helped that, at least, I still had Verna with me.

Mel and Verna began to take more than just a casual interest in each other. They seemed to be making eyes at each other and constantly flirting back and forth. I was somewhat jealous; Verna didn't seem to have much time for me.

I'm sure Morris didn't know what to do with Rocky and me at this point, but from all the packing, it was obvious we were moving somewhere. I had seen enough of California myself, and hoped we were going back to Texas.

That night we drove right past Disneyland without even slowing down. Like a lot of dreams, Disneyland faded from view out the back window.

The five of us were headed to Burlington, Colorado, Morris and Mel's home town. We did stop at a Justice of the Peace somewhere in New Mexico and Verna and "Uncle Mel" were married.

We had just crossed into Colorado when I decided I wanted answers to a few questions that had weighed heavy on my mind for hours.

"Morris,—why was my Mom arrested?"

He seemed to ignore me.

"How long will Mom be gone?"

"Are you writing a book?" he asked.

"Maybe," I answered, trying not to sound too much like a smart aleck.

"Then leave that chapter out." Morris smirked, glaring at me in the rearview mirror.

As you can see, I didn't. It serves him right for ignoring me.

CHAPTER
FOURTEEN

M orris and Mel's parents were living in Burlington, Colorado and we moved in with them. I called them Grandpa and Grandma Mac even though they weren't my real grandparents.

I was big for my age, and Grandpa Mac gave me my first lesson in what it was like to work for a living. He called it "earning my room and board."

Grandpa Mac had homesteaded 160 acres in the 1930's, south of Stratton, Colorado, near the North Fork of the Smoky Hill River. The "Dust Bowl" left his farm buried in dirt drifts and the Great Depression took what little was left. A hardy man, Grandpa Mac fought out an existence and stayed despite the hardships. After all else failed, he moved into Burlington and became the local garbage man. Using a wagon and team of horses, he made his rounds down the alleys.

I'm sure he took a lot of what he picked up to the town dump, but an amazing amount of items would come home with him each day. His yard was stacked high with scrap that he thought had some value.

He had retired from the trash route when we arrived in Burlington, but the huge piles of junk remained. Sometimes people would still stop by looking for this or that. It seemed like he had a complete inventory of everything in the junkyard stored in his brain, and knew exactly where he could find whatever they were looking for.

Besides owning a junkyard, he raised goats, chickens and pigs, all within the Burlington city limits. There were always chores to do before and after school, and we often didn't stop working until the sun went down in the evening. All the goats had to be milked by hand and the other animals fed and watered twice a day.

⟡

The months quickly passed and another school year started. It was always a rush to get the milking done and still make it to school on time. If being in a new school wasn't bad enough, the stigma of Mom being in prison and living in a junkyard added to my low self esteem.

It had been one of those rush mornings when my teacher called me to the front of the class. I couldn't think of anything I had done wrong.

Sniffing the air, the teacher said, "You smell like a goat." The teacher's words were loud enough for everyone in the classroom to hear.

"You get down to the gym and take a shower before you come back to this classroom."

I felt a knot in my throat the size of Texas. I tried to fight the tears back, but still felt them running down my cheeks. My face burned with embarrassment as my eyes blurred. I wanted to run, but I held my head high, as if the words didn't bother me. Glancing at the kids seated at their desks, I could see some of them smiling and heard others snickering as I went out the door. I considered just going home, but if Morris found out what happened he would probably kill the teacher. Besides, I was too embarrassed for anyone else to know.

As I undressed to shower, the janitor walked up with a strange look on his face. "What are you doing here? Why aren't you in class?"

Too embarrassed to answer him, I looked the other way and turned the water on. If he really wanted to continue his questions he would just have to get wet, because I wasn't going to look at him. With my luck he'll probably come back with the principal, I thought. I didn't want to talk, or face anyone.

Thankfully, when I finished showering the janitor had left the room. As much as I dreaded it, I would have to go back to the classroom and face the looks from the kids again.

I stood outside the classroom for a few minutes trying to build my courage. Taking a deep breath, I opened the door slowly. I hoped I could enter without anyone seeing me, but that wasn't possible. Again I was faced with a frown from the teacher and the snickers and smiles from some of the class. I felt sick in my stomach.

God only knows how much I wanted to be back in Bridge City. I wanted to run out of that school and never look back. The bitterness cut deep in my heart, and its taste was rotten. I walked away scarred, but a stronger and more caring person. I never wanted what happened to me to happen to any other kid. Ever!

All my experiences in school weren't horrible, but it's the bad ones that jump off the bookshelf of my memory. Kind of like a dark silhouette waiting to pounce at any moment. Each bad experience brought my self esteem lower. I had reached a point where I always wondered what the other kids thought when they looked at me. It was as if they could see right through me and knew my thoughts. After awhile, it has a way of eating away at your very soul.

While the other kids would gather on the ball field and pick each other for their teams, I would hang out on the opposite side of the building out of their sight. I could hear them laughing and cheering each other on. I ached to belong. I just couldn't allow myself to be subjected to teasing or the possibility of not being picked for a team. Besides that, it seemed like all the other kids owned their own ball gloves. All the boys proudly showed off their gloves and spent considerable time oiling and properly breaking them in. I can't help but wonder how much of a difference it may have made in my life if I had just owned that one item. It's hard to imagine something as small as a baseball glove making a difference in someone's life.

It wasn't like I didn't have friends. There were a few boys who were a lot like me. We just hung out together telling jokes or stories. Some of my friends were from dysfunctional families too. Like me, they lived in some of the poorer homes -- the wrong side of the tracks, as some people would say.

One cold winter day during recess, myself and three other boys were trying to hit sparrows perched on the top edge of the high school with snowballs. The building must have been four stories high, and it took a very strong arm and a well-compacted snowball to even come close to hitting a bird.

Just as I was taking my turn, the principal walked out on the fire escape. The snowball was already free of my hand, and its path toward the birds suddenly turned as if by some magical force. It hit the principle on the side of his head with a *splat*. Even from our position far below, we could see the red mark on the side of his face. To say he was furious would be an understatement. I didn't run, but I can't say I didn't think about it. Surely he knew it was an accident....

The principle came bouncing down the stairs, three steps at a time. Before I could even stop smiling and say, "I'm sorry," he was dragging me back up the fire escape to his office.

I think instead of being circumcised at birth, the doctor had removed the principal's sense of humor. He took a large wooden paddle that was hanging on the wall and made a lasting impression on me. Actually, it was more of a lasting impression on my butt that resembled the shape of his paddle, with little circles where he had previously drilled holes. I fought back my need to cry, as that would be considered an admission of weakness. I didn't want him to experience any additional pleasure from my beating. I wore the principal's brand for the next three days and hated that school even more.

I was so glad when spring arrived, and school was out for another summer. Even though the temperatures were warming up, Grandma had me cutting and stacking firewood and kindling to prepare for the next winter. There was an old outhouse that Grandma wanted stacked full of wood, from the floor to the roof.

We had a garden from hell that seemed to stretch on forever. In the summer months Grandpa had about an acre of potatoes that needed hoeing. Just when I finished the field it was time to start all over again. Later in the summer, Grandpa would cut the grass growing along Highway 24 with a horse drawn sickle and then we went back and raked it, using the team of horses for that job, too. I had to pick up those piles of hay with a pitch fork and load the wagon as high as possible.

Grandpa had a car parked in the yard but never drove it, preferring to use his team and wagon. Grandpa held to the old ways and did not enjoy progress. They had just never caught up to the modern world. People driving by looked at us in amazement, like we were from another place in time.

It was a lot of hard work for a young boy with the sun beating down on my head all day. When I complained about having to work so hard, Grandpa again reminded me that I was earning my room and board. Room and board were exactly what my living arrangements were. He had worked hard all his life and didn't see any reason why I shouldn't do the same. In spite of the hard working conditions, I never went hungry. Going to play with friends was something I didn't dare ask to do. Besides, I already knew what the answer would be.

There was a vast difference between this life style and what I had become accustomed to back in Texas. No hunting, fishing, swimming or roaming the country.

If I sassed back, as Grandma Mac called it, she would draw back her hand and threaten to box my ears.

Rocky and I weren't allowed to get down on our knees to play marbles because we would wear out the knees of our pants. Playing to Grandma Mac was nonsense. The only relief from our misery was each evening we were allowed to play checkers.

The main room in our house was a combination living room, kitchen and dining room all packed into one. It had a rocking chair, a china cabinet in one corner and in the center of the room a table with chairs. A large Majestic wood burning stove took up most of the remaining space. The stove also doubled as our heat source during the winter months. It had a water reservoir tank on one side that had to be filled by hand. By the time Grandma finished cooking a meal, the water would be steaming -- just right for washing the dishes when we were done eating. I would wash, and Rocky would dry.

On top of the china cabinet was a Zenith table radio with a badly frayed power supply cord. Its black dial covered three bands: Standard Broadcast, short-wave and police. I often studied the dial and longed to try out the police band or short wave but I wasn't allowed to touch the radio. On Saturday nights, Grandma Mac would turn the radio on and tune in station WSN and the Grand Ole Opry in Nashville. I could almost imagine myself sitting on the front row of the Ryman Auditorium and watching Roy Acuff and Patsy Cline perform live. Most mornings we would listen to the weather and Trading Post, but the rest of the time the radio stayed off to save electricity.

Other than a Bible, the only book in the house was an old geography edition, one of the few things I was allowed to touch. As I looked through the pages, I could almost visualize what it would be like to listen to countries all over the world on the radio. As I turned through the pages, I always stopped on a map of Texas. Closing my eyes, I would say a silent prayer while holding my finger on the map where Bridge City should be.

"God, please take me back to Texas. You have to know how much I hate it here. If you ask Grandma, I'm sure she will want me back. Amen."

❧

I didn't really expect Christmas to be much. A heavy snow was falling, though beautiful, it only added to my loneliness. Mom was in prison, and I was a thousand miles from where I really wanted to be.

To add to the holiday spirit, a Christmas card arrived from Box 160 Lansing, Kansas, with a bright red censored stamp across the top. Mom wrote about how much she missed us, and wished we could spend Christmas together. I knew what she did was wrong, but Christmas time in prison just didn't seem right.

While watching the snow pile up against the window of my room in the cold basement, I wrote this song.

CHRISTMAS TIME IN PRISON

A little boy came knocking
On the prison door
And as the warden let him in
His tears fell to the floor
He said it's Christmas time
And I'm lonely as can be
Oh please Mr. Warden
Let me take her home with me
For Christmas time in prison
Must be a lonely day
Please Mr. Warden
Don't make my Momma stay
Christmas time in prison
I know it can't be right
Oh please Mr. Warden
Let me take her home tonight
My dad has been waiting
Everyday that she's been gone
And now it's Christmas time
And I think she should be home
I know that she'll be good
If you set her free
So please Mr. Warden
Let me take her home with me
For Christmas time in prison
Must be a lonely day
Please Mr. Warden
Don't make my Momma stay
Christmas time in prison
I know it can't be right
Oh please Mr. Warden
Let me take her home tonight

You can only imagine the excitement when a local civic group showed up at our house a few day's before Christmas with a box of toys. Rocky and I tore into the box like dogs digging in the garbage.

Most of the things they gave us were more for a kid Rocky's age, including the girls yellow winter coat. Thank God it was too small for me! Unfortunately, poor Rocky had to wear it. After being teased a few times at school, he would hide the coat in the bushes in the morning, then after school, he would wear it home.

I was amazed when I saw a Remco toy radio station in the box. It was made to resemble a "real" radio station. I grabbed it from the box and moved away, announcing it was mine before Rocky could lay claim to it. Rocky could have everything else.

The radio station looked really fancy. It was made out of black and gray plastic with fake gold dials and gauges with a spotlight mounted on the top. A small telegraph key had a wire that plugged into the radio. There were no directions, but it couldn't be that hard to figure out.

Thoughts of contacting my family in Texas raced through my mind as I studied the dial. There had to be a way to contact them. After all, this was a radio station and Grandma and Big Mama listened to radio all the time. If I could figure out how to make it work, I could get them to come rescue me, I reasoned.

With a huge smile, I rushed my new found treasure to the basement and attempted to try it out. A sick feeling overcame me and moved to my stomach, when I discovered the radio station didn't have batteries.

With every ounce of courage I could muster, I trudged back upstairs. Taking a deep breath, I asked the life altering question; "Grandma, can we buy some batteries for my radio?"

"We don't have money for that nonsense," Grandma answered without hesitation.

"It just isn't fair!" I wanted to scream, but the cry stopped in the middle of my throat just as it had stopped so many times before. I ran back to the basement angry and fighting off tears. I wasn't giving up that easy. This was my lifeline to the outside world, my escape, and I was going to find a way to make the radio work.

All I needed was two "D" batteries but it may as well have been a thousand. I racked my brain trying to find a way to make the radio station work. All at once an idea hit me. An idea, but it was much more than that. A bursting kaleidoscope of thoughts exploded in my brain. It hung there almost blinding me with its light: A bare light bulb that hung from the rafters in the center of my bedroom. That's it! I'll hook it up to electricity. Logic told me that 120 volts would work much better than two "D" batteries. Not only could the signal reach Texas, but I guessed anywhere in the world.

With a knife I kept hidden in my room to fight off monsters, I cut the electrical cord off an old lamp I found abandoned in the basement. Carefully stripping the rubber and exposing the copper wires, I wrapped the bare wires around the battery contacts in the back of the radio station.

I knew this was my only hope of getting back to Bridge City. It had to work! I plugged the electrical cord into the wall outlet and was ready to test the telegraph key. Saying a silent prayer, I held my breath and pushed down the key that would connect me to the world.

There was a loud pop, a flash of light, and the smell of burnt rubber as smoke drifted up from the back of my radio station. In just one big flash, it was all over. My hopes and dreams floated out the window and vanished in the smoke of the gloomily lit basement.

Rocky didn't have it as bad as I did, but then Grandma and Grandpa Mac were his real grandparents. To me living there was like a prison camp and I wanted out. I imagined even my Mom didn't have it as bad as I did, and she was in a real prison. I had to escape—that's all there was to it.

I shared my runaway plans with a few trusted friends and offered to let them come with me if they wanted. Most of my friends had good parents and nice homes with no reason to go, other than for the adventure, but two friends who had horses agreed to go.

I amended my runaway plan from riding a freight train to going by horseback. We could do like the cowboys from the Old West and ride the horses all the way to Texas, and then take jobs as cowboys on a ranch. During recess, that's all we talked about. I had become obsessed with the idea. We researched how many miles a horse could travel in a day and what supplies to take. It was only about a thousand miles and we could easily make it there in one summer. If nothing else, our math and geography skills were improving from all our research.

I found a map showing the Dodge City Trail in a library book. Carefully I tore out the page when no one was looking. That night I marked the watering holes and camp spots we could use on the way south to the Red River Valley on the

Texas/Oklahoma border. From there I figured we could go cross country to the head waters of the Sabine River, and then just keep working our way downstream toward the Gulf of Mexico. I even had a ranch picked out near Cow Bayou that I was sure would hire "experienced" cowboys.

The harder I worked on the idea the closer the time for our escape came. It seemed like we had everything in place. I smiled at the thought of riding down the dry wash of the Smoky Hill River with a warm breeze blowing through my hair. Camping by our fire at night and listening to the coyotes howl at the end of a long day, it was going to be a great trip, and I couldn't wait to get started.

The week before we planned to leave, Morris found a job working as a carpenter's helper for one of my friend's dads. When payday came on Friday, he celebrated his new job and left for a night on the town. Actually, I don't think he needed a reason to celebrate. It's just something he did any time he had money.

I awoke to the bright bare light bulb shining above my bed and the sound of Morris yelling at the top of his lungs.

"Get your ass out of bed right now. We're going to talk."

I jumped to my feet, but he pushed me back down on the bed. I could tell he was drunk, but I'd never seen him this mad at me before.

"I hear you don't like it here, and you're planning to run away. Is that true?"

I sat numbly on the side of the bed staring at the floor.

"Yes sir," I answered, afraid he was going to punch me with his doubled up fists.

"If you want to go back to Texas that damn bad, then by God I'll find a way for you to get there."

Morris stormed up the basement stairs as I sat there on the side of the bed shaking. When I knew it was safe and he wasn't coming back, I knelt down on the cold cement floor and prayed:

"Thank you God, for answering my prayers."

Yes! I'm going back to Texas!

The timing was just right as Uncle Mel needed to relocate to find work. Aunt Verna must have suggested they go to Bridge City. After they talked to Morris, he agreed they could take me with them. One of my friends must have snitched me out, and told someone about my runaway plans, but it didn't matter. It couldn't have worked out any better if I had planned it this way. Still, I couldn't help wonder what the trip would have been like by freight train or horseback.

Mel, Verna and I left Burlington early in the morning and we sang songs almost the whole way. When we crossed the Texas state line, it had just rained and we could smell the scent of sage blowing in through the vent on Uncle Mel's old Mercury. We sang; *"Deep In The Heart of Texas"* for the next ten miles. There were no trees, just mile after mile of range-land as far as I could see. It was nothing like the part of Texas I called home, but I was both proud and glad to be there.

I couldn't wait to get back to Bridge City, throw my shoes away, and feel mud squishing between my toes again.

I t was raining in Bridge City the morning of June 27, 1957 when I woke up. The aroma of brewing Seaport Coffee filled the house. All night long, Grandma had been listening to radio reports on Hurricane Audrey. She was about to hit land. The radio listed Bridge City as an area that should evacuate to higher ground, but Grandma said we were staying.

"I've been through a lot of these over the years. Just have faith in God. He'll protect us." Grandma spoke with such confidence, I wasn't worried in the least.

Our neighborhood looked like a ghost town. The rain was coming down so hard it blocked the view of the police car patrolling through the neighborhood with a bull horn giving everyone their final evacuation warning.

The radio again warned this was a big one, and everyone should evacuate while you still can. I looked at Grandma, and she gave me a slight smile.

"We'll be fine," she reassured me. We didn't have a car to leave even if she had changed her mind.

A loud clap of thunder boomed across the heavens, and shook the whole house, announcing Hurricane Audrey's arrival. Grandma opened both the front and back doors, as floods of horizontal rain blew in on the floor.

"You see," she told me, "If we don't open things up the air pressure will cause the house to explode." Now that was a comforting thought, just when I thought we didn't have anything to worry about.

After she propped the doors open with my custom-made cypress knee door stops, the skies grew even darker. It was apparent the hurricane was going to hit full force. I stood at the back door watching the sky, my adrenaline pumping. Thunder and lightning jolted me to the realization that we could die. Torrents of rain blew in, passing through our house then right out the front, causing the whole structure to shake on its foundation. Most people would panic at a time like this, but for me it was totally the opposite. Grandma didn't really seem that worried about it herself, so why should I? I would glance at Grandma when a gust of wind shook the house, but she just kept reading her Bible in the dim light.

"Grandma, come look. The neighbor's doghouse and part of a shed is floating down our ditch and our footbridge just washed away." My excitement didn't faze her. She just kept reading her Bible. Even though a hurricane was blowing through our house, she had calmness about her.

"Son, the Bible says if we have the faith of a mustard seed, we can move a mountain. So why should we worry about a hurricane?"

"I'm not worried Grandma, but I sure wish we had a boat. Just in case," I answered.

Just to prove my faith, I took my shirt off and stood just inside the house near the open door and leaned into the wind, getting completely drenched.

"Cliff, the Bible says not to tempt the Lord thy God. Now you get back away from that door," Grandma scolded.

There was no argument from me. Grandma got up occasionally to mop the water off the floor. I settled for looking outside through the closed window.

I was amazed to see a large lake growing in size all around us. Not only was it a lake, but it looked like a powerful river with a current. A propane tank was floating down the ditch behind our house, like it had an outboard motor hooked to it.

It's a good thing our house was raised up on blocks, as I'm sure that feature kept the flood waters from getting in. The ground was so saturated with water, and the wind so strong, it knocked large oak trees down everywhere. Some of them had stood for a hundred years or more, and they were blown down with huge splashes as they fell into this hurricane-made lake. It really bothered Grandma, because many of the trees were the oaks that her dad had planted when she was a little girl.

As the eye of Hurricane Audrey reached us, the storm loosened its grip on Bridge City, and the sky instantly turned a beautiful blue. The sun came out and birds were flying everywhere. Snakes were jam-packed on debris floating in the water.

I was surprised that Grandma let me go out while the hurricane's eye was over Bridge City. I doubt she knew how bad the snakes were. Ray Simmons was outside, too, walking around the neighborhood in the waist deep water surveying the damage. Grandma warned me not to go far, and when it started getting cloudy again, I better get my tail back in the house. She said the second part of the hurricane was supposed to be worse.

Ray and I started catching snakes and putting them in a gunny sack. It was almost ridiculous to be standing in the water as deep as your belly button and have a mad snake swimming right toward you. Just before it was close enough to bite, Ray would grab the snake and add it to the sack. Most of the snakes were venomous water moccasins, but we found a few we couldn't identify. Before it started getting dark again, we had almost a gunnysack full.

Ray's dad helped us hang the gunnysack full of snakes from his clothesline. With several blasts from his shotgun, pieces of dead snakes littered the yard.

The eye had passed and the second half of the hurricane was hitting us full force as I ran for the safety of home. Grandma was standing on the front steps looking for me as I came into the yard, pushing knee deep water ahead of me.

Just as Grandma had predicted, the second half of the hurricane was much worse. The wind and rain came fast and furiously. The lake that surrounded our house was almost even with the opening of our door

When the winds died down, we heard on the radio that Cameron, Louisiana, just thirty-five air miles away was almost completely wiped out. The announcer said that volunteers were desperately needed to help the survivors.

When the water had receded enough for traffic to return to Bridge City, Big Mama and Papaw drove into the driveway. I don't know where they had weathered the storm, but they were both drunk. I believe that it was Big Mama and Papaw who came up with the idea of having hurricane parties.

They too, had heard about the devastation of Cameron on the radio and had come by to pick me up. They intended to drive to Cameron to see what we could do there to help. Grandma knew they were too drunk to be driving, much less in any condition to help anyone. From the radio reports we were receiving, Grandma didn't think Cameron was any place for a nine year old boy.

I really wanted to go, but Grandma gave me the same look she had on her face when Uncle Rudy wanted to take me alligator hunting. That look was enough to stop me cold in my tracks and I didn't argue with her.

It's really fortunate that I couldn't go, because the rescue operation turned into a body recovery, and not something I would want to remember. The hurricane had killed 425 people, 154 of who were under the age of nine years old. Hurricane Audrey became one of the deadliest hurricanes in the history of the United States.

CHAPTER

SEVENTEEN

I kept bouncing back and forth between Big Mama's and Grandma's. After a lot of discussion between them, it was decided I needed to be settled in one place before school started again. Big Mama and Papaw would be my lucky custodians. I didn't care whom I lived with. I was just glad someone wanted me.

Big Mama and Papaw moved from the house on Sabine Lake to a little shack in Louisiana on the banks of the Sabine River. The house was across the river from Deweyville, Texas and Bridge City was only twenty three miles away.

It seemed like Big Mama and Papaw always picked really great places to live, and this house was no exception. There is an indescribable magic I can't explain about living beside a river that has flowed over 500 miles and is about to end its long journey in the Gulf of Mexico.

The house wasn't much to look at, but that wasn't important to me. What did matter was an old row boat that was abandoned in the swamp behind our house. The faded name of "Cajun Queen" was hand painted on the sides.

I spent a lot of days entertaining myself on that little body of water catching soft shell turtles that Big Mama would make into a delicious turtle soup. It made me feel important to be helping with our daily food supply. As Grandpa Mac back in Burlington would say, I was "earning my room and board."

Though we lived in Louisiana, there wasn't a school close by, except for the one in Deweyville, Texas. The principal explained to Big Mama that living in one state and going to school in another wasn't common practice.

"You're not taxpayers in our state, so I'm not sure I can allow him to attend," he said, with a hint of sarcasm.

That was fine with me. Maybe I wouldn't have to go to school at all. I was starting to like living in Louisiana even more.

"Not taxpayers! You son-of-a-bitch, let me tell you something! My husband was in World War II and he had seven ships blown out from under him, and you have the gall to tell us we're not taxpayers. He had the shit shot out of him fighting for this country. Now you're sitting here on your fat ass telling me that my grandson can't go to your goddamn school, because we live on the wrong side of the river?"

I thought Big Mama was going to climb over his desk and hit him. It didn't take too much persuading before she convinced the principal that I would be going to school in Deweyville.

⚭

Half a mile down the highway into Louisiana was a bar that Big Mama and Papaw went to quite frequently. It seemed like we would spend more time there than we did at home. The customers were always handing me quarters to play the Jukebox. Sometimes I stood there for hours, watching the records spin and memorizing songs. I enjoyed making the customers groan by playing the same song six times in a row. I wondered why none of the people at the bar had kids. If they did, why didn't they bring them so I'd have someone to play with? It got awful lonesome hanging out there all day with nothing to do, but complaining didn't help.

Often I would go out behind the bar and sit in the shadow of the building, spending hours throwing rocks into the swamp and wishing. Wishing Big Mama and Papaw didn't drink so much and my Mom wasn't in prison. Wishing I could live with Grandma in Bridge City. Wishing I could just go home.

❦

There was a home that looked like an old houseboat across the highway from where we lived. It looked like the river had deposited it on the bank after a flood, and it had remained there after the water receded.

Big Mama had noticed a boy outside near the house on one of our trips home from the bar. Recognizing my need to have friends, she insisted I go over and invite this boy to our house to play.

Bashfully, I approached their house and a big black dog ran out to meet me growling. A half dozen heads poked out the door and one of them called the dog back into the house. I don't think they had ever had a visitor before by the way they acted. A boy who looked a year or two older than me came outside, curiously looking me over.

"What do you want?" he asked, with a frown.

With social skills like that, I could tell he had been on the wrong side of the river an awfully long time.

"Can you come over to my house and play?" I bravely asked.

I almost expected him to say no and sic the dog on me. The boy looked junk-yard-dog-tough with freckles covering his face and a few teeth missing.

"I guess," he answered after looking back over his shoulder at his mom to see if she disapproved.

He seemed just as nervous as he followed me across the highway to my house. I'm sure he was wondering what we were going to do, and I wasn't sure myself. I didn't have toys or games. Maybe we could shoot my BB gun or I could give him a tour of the swamp behind our house. I could always check my fish trap and show him how I catch turtles. It sure felt awkward with him walking behind me saying nothing. Occasionally I looked over my shoulder to see if he was still there. Making eye contact, I would quickly turn around and keep walking with him about six paces behind me. I'm sure he felt like he was being led into some kind of trap.

Big Mama had a plan that would help break the ice and shared it with us, when my new friend and I walked in the door. She had pulled two pairs of old boxing gloves out of a trunk and announced we were going to learn how to box.

This boy had to be a full foot taller than I was. I was quick to let Big Mama know that I didn't want to fight. Of course Big Mama had to call me a sissy and cry baby. She told me it would be nice to have a son who was as tough as this boy was. I think he was embarrassed too. He stood there saying nothing with the boxing gloves on, unsure what to do. Big Mama was directing the fight and the boy didn't really have any more control than I did. She staggered toward us and took his arm, hitting me in the head with his glove, trying to force us to fight.

She got her way, and we exchanged a few punches, but he kicked my butt! His first solid punch knocked me down. Big Mama yelled for me to get back up and fight. Just when I was up on my feet again, his punch took me back down. This time it was really hard to see where he was through my tears. Big Mama called me a sissy again and pulled me back to my feet, shoving me back toward him.

Finally I breathed a sigh of relief when the boy said he had to go home. I never saw him again after that, and I dang sure didn't go there and invite him over again. I'm sure he must have thought we were really strange people, but then again, I guess maybe we were.

✿

We had been at the bar all afternoon one sultry Saturday. I had begged and hounded Big Mama for over an hour about when we could go home.

"Why don't you play another game of shuffle board? Do you really want to go home to that hot house?" she asked, handing me another quarter. Of course I did, or I wouldn't have asked.

Big Mama often used the fact that the bar had a big air cooler as a reason to hang out there. Cooled air, other than an overworked osculating fan wasn't a luxury we had at home. I admit it felt good, but I didn't want to spend the day at the bar, just because it's cooler there. Big Mama was getting a little annoyed at me and finally agreed we could go.

She wasn't in the best mood when we arrived home. We

walked in the door and discovered a big ugly cat on the kitchen counter eating Big Mama's corn bread. I could see the fire in Big Mama's eyes as she threw her purse across the room, cussing at the fleeing cat.

Big Mama quickly blocked the cat's path and closed the windows so it couldn't escape. We chased it all over the house. Finally we backed it into the corner of the bathroom where Big Mama was able to catch it.

"Get rid of it," Big Mama yelled, as she handed the clawing beast to me.

"What do you want me to do with it?" I asked, as it struggled to free itself.

"Just take it out on the bridge and throw the damn thing in the river. I guarantee it won't be eating from our table again," Big Mama scorned.

Papaw fiercely objected to her making me do this; telling us a story about how a cat had once saved his life. He was serving on a ship during World War II, when a cat came up to him and appeared hungry. He told the cat; "Stay right here and I'll bring you something to eat." Papaw went inside the ship and soon heard an explosion on the deck. It turned out a shell fired by the enemy had landed right where he had been standing.

Big Mama wasn't the least bit impressed in his old war stories and handed me the cat as it struggled to free itself from my grasp.

"Get the damn thing out of here right now!" Big Mama yelled. It was a power struggle between Papaw and Big Mama with me in the middle, as they argued the cat's fate.

"Do what I say," she repeated as I just stood there with the cat in my arms waiting to see who would win their argument.

Maybe she was just testing me to see if I would do everything she told me to, but really it was more than that. Big Mama turned really mean when she was drunk, and Papaw and I both knew that.

I'd never killed anything larger than birds with my BB gun, and I really didn't feel right about doing this. I knew that arguing with Big Mama was hopeless.

Talking quietly to the purring cat, I carried it to the bridge.

"I'm sorry, I don't want to do this but Big Mama said I have to. If you hadn't got in the house and ate our cornbread, you wouldn't be in this mess. Don't look at me with those big brown eyes. This is all your fault!"

I tried to justify in my own mind why I had to carry out the death sentence on a poor hungry cat. Walking toward the center of the bridge, I looked down at the brown water about thirty feet below; small eddies swirled like miniature tornadoes.

A log truck blasted his air horn, warning me to move closer to the railing as he roared past me in a blur. The sound startled me, causing me to jump and the cat to dig its claws into my arm as it leaped to the pavement.

Looking back toward our house, I tried to see if Big Mama was watching. Surely the truck's air horn brought her to the window, but it was hard to tell if she was there or not. If she didn't see the cat drop, I would really be in deep trouble.

My arm was covered with raised red scratch marks and droplets of blood. Desperately I chased the cat down the highway toward the Louisiana side of the bridge, the whole time hoping Big Mama wasn't watching. If it came back to the house, I could just tell Big Mama it must have swam back to shore. She was probably too drunk to see that far anyway.

Big Mama stood in the doorway with her hands on her hips, watching me walk back down the driveway.

"Did you throw it in the river," Big Mama asked, as if by some remote chance I would disobey her.

"Yes Ma'am," I lied, showing her the scratch marks on my arms.

The next day the cat was back at our house. Big Mama didn't say anything so maybe she was just too drunk to remember what she told made me do. I sure wasn't going to bring it up.

✵

I was shocked one evening when Big Mama said that I was driving home. The sun was dropping behind the loblolly pines, and casting long shadows across the gravel parking lot in front of the bar. I couldn't believe she was really going to let me drive. I couldn't even reach the gas or brake pedals.

Papaw took his toolbox out of the back of the pickup and placed it on the seat so I could sit high enough to see out the windshield. Big Mama was sitting in the middle next to me, and told me just to steer, she would take care of the clutch, brakes and gas pedal. I think they were just too drunk to drive, and thought I had a better chance of getting us home.

The drive west on Highway 12 was going fine. I was able to stay within my lane except for one near miss with a truck. As we approached the Sabine River Bridge and the turn off for our driveway, I started to panic. I wasn't an experienced driver, but I could tell Big Mama was going much to fast for me to make the corner.

"Turn!" Big Mama yelled, grabbing the steering wheel and cranking it hard to the right. Trying to stomp on the brake pedal, she hit the gas instead. The old Chevy pickup went into a skid, the tires squealing beneath us.

Her scream told me we were in serious trouble. I stared out the front windshield, and then shot a quick glance down the embankment at the river, my heart pounding. I could see it coming, but there was no way to stop it. To my horror we went over the side of the embankment, careening down toward the river and sure death.

The pickup was just starting to roll over on its side when it wedged against a concrete marker that was sticking up.

We came to rest at such a steep angle that Big Mama and Papaw slid down to my side of the seat with all their weight against me. I could hardly breathe but was able to pull the door handle, causing the door to swing open, spilling all three of us out of the truck. I had a death grip on the door. Big Mama and Papaw tumbled past me, all the way to the bottom where they came to rest on the muddy river bank.

No one was hurt, but Big Mama was too drunk to climb back up to the road. Papaw and I tried to help her up the embankment, but she eventually quit trying and flopped down in the weeds and mud. Papaw sent me home with instructions to bring back a pillow and a blanket.

When I returned, Papaw had moved Big Mama to a sandbar beside the river. She had passed out so he just covered her up and sat down beside her, letting her sleep it off there. It was getting dark and the mosquitoes were out in full force, so I climbed back up to our house. They would probably both spend the night of the river bank, I reasoned.

The loneliness and silence in the house was overpowering. I watched out the window, half expecting Big Mama and Papaw to come staggering up our driveway, but it didn't happen.

The next morning when Big Mama and Papaw came home, they were both covered in mud and mosquito bites. The pickup stayed hanging on the side of the embankment and Papaw worried that a cop would show up asking questions. Papaw washed up the best he could, but didn't have clean clothes to change into. In spite of his soiled clothes, he walked to Deweyville and hired someone to retrieve our pickup.

It took two wreckers to get the pickup back up on the road. One was hooked on to the side to keep it from tumbling down to the river, and the other pulled the truck up at an angle toward our driveway.

Big Mama spent the morning washing clothes with an old ringer type washing machine on the back porch. She had the shakes and got her fingers a little too close to the ringer as she was feeding in the wet clothes. Her whole arm was quickly sucked in all the way to her elbow, and the rollers just sat there bouncing up and down on her arm.

I started giggling but was soon laughing so hard my face hurt as she screamed for help from Papaw. He ran into the room to see what was going on and quickly reversed the rollers so that slowly her arm came back out. When things calmed down, she looked over at me. "What in the hell were you laughing about?" She yelled.

"I was thinking how funny it would be if the whole top of the washing machine started spinning round and round while your hand was caught and you had to jump over the washing machine each time it went around." I started laughing again, just picturing that in my mind.

"I'll slap the snot out of you!" she yelled.

Her arm came up as she started to carry out her threat, but it hurt her to much to move. It allowed me time to run off laughing.

Sometimes a thought would enter my mind and I couldn't control myself. I would laugh for what appeared to others as no reason at all. My devious little mind seemed to always be thinking.

I don't know if the owner of the property discovered we were living in the house illegally or if Big Mama and Pawpaw really rented the place and just forgot about paying the rent. I do know one day the owner showed up and told us we had to move. There was no 30 day eviction process. We were completely loaded and moved out within a few hours.

CHAPTER

EIGHTEEN

Big Mama and Papaw were obsessed with the idea of moving to Arkansas. A retiree's paradise, they called it, and with no where to live, talk of moving to Arkansas became even more frequent. The three of us were living with Grandma in Bridge City.

"I'm sick and tired of all these damn mosquitoes, the high humidity, and the holier-than-thou attitude Bible thumping neighbors," Big Mama snapped.

If the wind was from the north, she complained about the smell of the pulp plant at Woodville, up in Tyler County. It seemed like every time Big Mama started drinking at least one of her complaints about Bridge City would come up. Her biggest pet peeve was always the snooping neighbors. She claimed they were so damn nosey they knew what we ate, when we went to the bathroom and even what brand of toilet paper we wiped our ass with.

Big Mama and Papaw asked me if I wanted to go with them, or I could stay with Grandma if I wanted. After they told me about the mountains in Arkansas and how great the fishing and hunting would be, it was an easy decision to make. I'm sure they told me a dozen other reasons why it was a better place to live, but it was settled. I was going.

Just after Papaw's retirement check arrived, we told Grandma good bye. She didn't cry like she did before. Maybe she knew we would be back.

Our pickup was loaded with all our possessions and headed for Arkansas. Big Mama and Papaw were already drunk and it wasn't even noon yet. I sat in the middle between the two of them as they chained smoked, wishing I could hold my breath until we got there. I knew that would be impossible.

"Can I ride in the back?" I asked.

"No, there's no room back there. Now you sit still, we have a long way to go," Big Mama answered without looking at me. She had both hands on the steering wheel in a death grip and flinched with each bump.

We hadn't gone any distance before we approached a bridge. Big Mama always had a great fear of hitting a bridge rail and going over the side, only to die in a watery grave. I don't think the thought of head on collisions bothered her, as she would always drive in the middle when we crossed bridges. To be safe, she would straddle the middle lane, long before she got to the bridge.

This time she chose to take the middle just as an oil company truck was trying to pass us. I heard his brakes squeal and the horn honking, but it didn't seem to bother Big Mama at all. She didn't even look back.

"Big Mama, you almost made us wreck," I warned.

Without answering, she gave me a look that told me I better shut up.

We continued on down the middle of the bridge, doing at least 35 miles per hour, with the oil company truck almost pushing our rear bumper. As I looked back, the driver was shaking his fist at me.

"Big Mama, those men behind you act like they're really mad. I think they want to pass us."

"That's exactly why I want out of this damn state. Everyone's in a hurry to go somewhere and no one has any consideration for anyone else. Things will be a lot different in Arkansas."

When the man behind us had a chance to pass, I noticed the passenger in the truck writing down our license plate number. I told Big Mama and she yelled obscenities out the window as he went around us. Of course nothing she ever did was her fault when she was drinking.

We stopped at the first rest area we came to and spent a couple of hours there. While Big Mama and Papaw napped, I played in the creek and explored the Piney Hills.

It seemed like it took most of the day before we entered the city limits of Jasper, Texas. I spotted a drive in restaurant and asked if we could stop for an ice cream cone. Big Mama and Papaw both waited in the pickup while I went inside and waited in line to place my order. I was glad they decided not to come in with me, as the place was crowded with customers escaping the summer heat. As I waited in line I could see Big Mama and Papaw both taking turns drinking from their bottle, its contents protected from view by the brown paper bag.

As the waiter made my ice cream cone, the red lights of a police car parked behind our pickup caught my attention. Everyone in the drive-in was looking outside as Big Mama and Papaw were arrested. Of course Big Mama wouldn't go without a fight. Should I go outside? It would be embarrassing if the people watching even knew I was with them.

I stood watching through the window, as the officers put them both in handcuffs. Big Mama made one last attempt to kick the officer, but lost her balance and fell backwards, landing in a sitting position. That caused everyone watching to laugh.

"Boy is that lady hammered," one of the customers in a booth commented.

Papaw was placed in the back seat of the patrol car, but it took both officers to carry Big Mama to the other patrol car.

Big Mama or Papaw must have told the officers about me because soon they came inside and started asking me questions. I felt like every eye in the place was watching me … and listening. What had been a noisy drive-in restaurant was now quiet, except for a few whispers.

"Where were you folks headed to?" the officer asked.

Before I could even answer, the other police officer added; "Do you have any kin around here?"

"No sir, just my Grandma in Bridge City and my Aunt Gwen lives in Port Arthur," I answered.

It was really embarrassing as every face in the restaurant was focused on me. Their scrutiny was agonizing. The frustrations of living at this level of society bothered me. It wasn't long before another police car arrived. I was relieved to be taken away from the prying eyes to the Jasper County Court House.

The police officers must have found a phone number for Aunt Gwen because they told me she was driving up from Port Arthur to pick me up. Aunt Gwen had never been an option for a place to live because she was raising seven kids of her own. I was surprised she even had a phone.

I had heard so many negative things about the police from Big Mama, that I was worried. She would panic anytime she saw a patrol car when she was driving. When Mom was arrested in California, Morris had a few choice words about the cops too. He said they beat the shit out of him one time when he was arrested in Houston. I was surprised how nice the officers were to me. They took me out for supper to a nice restaurant in a hotel near the court house, complete with an ice cream sundae for dessert.

I avoided looking at the other guests as they asked the officer's what kind of horrendous crime I had committed. It was embarrassing to have to listen to the officer's explanations, and then the peoples eyes would fall back on me with that; Oh you poor little boy—wrong side of the river look. I was really starting to hate that look and the feelings that accompanied it.

Later that night the officers were sitting on a bench outside the courthouse with me, as we continued to wait for my aunt to come. One of the officers put his hand on my shoulder and patted me on the head with his other hand. The quiet of the night was broken by Big Mama screaming at the top of her lungs from the jail window.

"Get your hands off that boy you son-of-a-bitch! I saw you hit him you rotten bastard. You think you're a big man beating on a little boy. Why don't you come up here and try that with someone your own size? I'll kick your ass if you touch that boy again," she shrilled.

Her yelling caused the other prisoners to start their own campaign of obscenities. One male voice boomed out louder than all the others.

"Would you all just shut the hell up? I'm trying to sleep."

I wanted to crawl under the bench I was sitting on but Big Mama would have sworn the officer had knocked me out. I tried to yell back up to her that I was all right, he didn't hit me, but she was still screaming at the top of her lungs.

"Run Cliff, don't let the sons-of-bitches catch you."

The officers decided it would be better if we all sat where she couldn't see us, but it didn't seem to matter. Big Mama continued to scream and curse for the next hour. Eventually she must have gone to sleep or passed out. Aunt Gwen arrived late that night and took me back to Bridge City to live with Grandma.

CHAPTER

NINETEEN

About a month later, Big Mama and Papaw were out of jail and back in Bridge City. Their conversations still centered on just one thing: Getting out of Texas and moving to Arkansas. Big Mama studied the Texaco map daily and planned to cross to the Louisiana side of the river at Orange. As she put it; "I don't want to give those ass holes in Jasper another chance."

When Papaw's check arrived, our pickup was already loaded. After telling Grandma good bye *again,* we were on the way. We crossed the Sabine River at Orange and were into Louisiana in just a few minutes. In just a short while we were headed north out of the swamp lands and into the rolling hills and pine trees of western Louisiana.

Aunt Gwen and Uncle Willie had moved from Port Arthur to Evans, Louisiana, and Big Mama decided we would drive as far as their house the first day and stay the night with them.

I was hoping we could spend a few days there so I could play with my seven cousins but Uncle Willie didn't approve of Big Mama and Papaw's drinking. We were back on the highway to Arkansas early the next day. By the time we reached the Arkansas state line, Big Mama and Papaw were both too drunk to be driving, but we kept going.

It seemed like the more they drank, the more cigarettes they smoked. This was before anyone came up with the idea that second-hand smoke may be harmful. I had grown to hate the odor as it oozed about, filling the cab of our pickup. Fresh air rushing in the window was always a relief, but it never lasted long enough. If I complained too much about my eyes burning, Big Mama would call me a baby and suggest that maybe I should have stayed at Grandma's. The inside of our windows were covered with a haze from all the smoke, thick enough that I could draw pictures with my fingernails.

Even worse than the smell was the discomfort I often suffered when the butts they tossed out the window blew back and caused ashes to get into my eyes. God only knows how many times I prevented a fire when I pointed out burns in the seat before they grew too large.

Big Mama sometimes bought me candy cigarettes made to look like the real thing. The end was red or orange to resemble a glowing lit cigarette. They knew how much I hated the real thing, why would I want to imitate what I found so disgusting? I guess I'll never understand their thinking. Why not make candy hypodermic syringes for kid's whose parents are drug addicts, I wondered?

Big Mama had been driving since we left Shreveport, and Papaw was passed out on the passenger side before we reached the Arkansas line. Though I brought the state-line crossing to her attention, there was no fanfare like I expected.

Soon we entered the small town Fouke, Arkansas, on Highway 71 where a construction crew was doing road work. A road grader was working down a pile of gravel that a dump truck had just piled in the center of the road, the dust still thick in the air.

Big Mama's eyes seemed to be glazed over, almost unaware we had even entered a town, her speed never changed. Glancing at the speedometer, I could see we were still doing 35 miles per hour. This was unusual for Big Mama because she normally slowed down to 10 miles per hour for towns. Maybe the dust contributed to her poor vision, but she drove straight into that pile of gravel like it wasn't even there. Her head bounced off the steering wheel, and blood began flowing from her split lip.

Fortunately, her low speed didn't cause too much damage to the pickup. Big Mama pulled herself from the truck and staggered toward the construction crew, cussing them and some of the on-lookers, as she wiped the dripping blood from her lip. "Why in the hell don't you have someone flagging traffic?" She yelled at anyone that would listen.

The construction crew was standing there with their mouths open in disbelief, while their supervisor, his face beet red, yelled back at her. "Lady, can't you see that huge pile of gravel? If you can't see the gravel pile, you damn sure should have seen the road grader. Are you drunk or what?"

"You'll think drunk, you ignorant son-of-a-bitch," Big Mama yelled back, as she raised her fist and started walking toward him, ready to punch his lights out. Papaw was already out of the truck and grabbed her arms, holding her back.

"Get back in the damn truck right now. Do you want to go to jail?" Papaw yelled.

The construction boss calmed down after Papaw talked to him. I was too far away to hear their conversation, but whatever Papaw said worked.

Papaw and I tried pushing the truck backwards with all our strength as Big Mama popped the clutch, but she kept killing the motor. Finally the construction crew walked up, each finding a place to push and practically lifted our pickup off the gravel pile. Papaw and I jumped in as Big Mama jammed it into low gear and the truck jumped forward. The construction boss was shaking his head with a look of disgust as Big Mama drove past him, and raised her middle finger in his direction.

We continued on down the highway, as Big Mama held the steering wheel with her left hand and Papaw passed her the pint of whiskey to calm her nerves. She was still swerving in her lane, but hitting the gravel pile had made her a little more cautious.

We soon entered Texarkana and the highway turned into State Line Avenue, marking the boundary between Arkansas and Texas. It seemed strange to have traveled such a great distance and have Texas just across the center of the street from us.

As Big Mama drove passed a school, I was lost in thought. I wondered if all the schools in Arkansas were that big. I didn't say anything, but I hoped wherever I had to go to school would be small.

I shot to attention when I heard a loud crash that sounded like the pickup was falling apart. The noise continued as we traveled down the street, sounding almost like a tail pipe or muffler dragging but much louder. The noise woke Papaw, and he was yelling at Big Mama to just stop the damn thing. People were pointing and waving, but Big Mama just kept driving with the pickup making that horrible sound. I looked around as a car sped around us honking its horn and pointing. The car stopped in front of us, forcing Big Mama to come to a halt. A man jumped out and run back to our vehicle yelling at Big Mama in a panicked voice.

"Didn't you see that cop? You ran over him! He's stuck under your truck," the man screamed.

Big Mama's dark complexion turned pale, and her hands began to tremble violently. Her voice was quivering; she could barely speak.

"I'm sorry—I just didn't see him," she replied in tears.

"Damn it," Papaw mumbled, shaking his head side to side.

I wanted to get out and look but Papaw told me to stay in the truck. Big Mama was taking deep breaths and appeared to be on the verge of a nervous breakdown. Papaw and the man who had stopped us were down on their hands and knees reaching under our pickup trying to free the cop.

A crowd of onlookers gathered around watching and gossiping. Their sour looks and finger pointing again reminded me I was from the wrong side of the river. I hated it.

I sat there in silence, too embarrassed and afraid to look around. I prayed for the police officer wedged under our pickup. Only a miracle could save him. After all, we had traveled over a block after Big Mama hit him. Several police cars showed up with their red lights and sirens screaming.

"I got him," one of the men reaching under our truck announced.

I cringed as I heard him scraping against the bottom of the pickup as they struggled to free the officer. There were no screams or crying. His silence could only mean one thing; He had to be dead. As they pulled him out from under our pickup, I looked down, fully expecting to see blood, gore and the most horrific injuries a young boy could imagine.

To my pleasant surprise and relief, the men pulled out a badly mangled, metal, Coca-Cola Cop from under our pickup. Big Mama had run over the Coca-Cola Cop that was smack-dab in the center of the street and didn't even see it. The Coca-Cola Company made a sign that looked like a school crossing guard and placed in school zones to help protect children. It looked like a police officer, holding one hand in the air signaling to slow down. He held a sign in his other hand saying "SLOW School Zone." On the back it advertised Coca-Cola. It stood about five feet tall and had a base that allowed it to stand upright in the middle of the street.

This time Big Mama didn't resist when she was placed under arrest. I'm sure she was relived that she hadn't killed someone.

Papaw was placed under arrest too. The officer directed him to place his hands on the trunk of the patrol car.

"Spread your feet apart," the officer ordered as he started to pat him down.

Papaw either didn't understand what the officer wanted him to do, or he was just being hard headed.

"I said get your feet apart, the officer yelled as he kicked the inside of Papaw's boot. He had a surprised look on his face when he heard a clink.

"Damn it! Would you stop it? You're going to break my bottle!" Papaw groaned.

"Why didn't you tell me that was there?" The officer asked.

"I was hoping you wouldn't find it and I could take it to jail with me," Papaw answered with a frown.

"I don't know where you're from, but it doesn't work that way in Arkansas," the officer grumbled as he stuffed Papaw in the back seat of a waiting patrol car.

I was placed in a third police car and rode in silence to the court house. I don't remember the charges, but we were all immediately taken before a judge. After a lot of legal talk, Big Mama and Papaw were told to stand before the judge. Scared to death, I sat at attention on the front row. I can't remember all the legal jargon that was discussed in the court room, but I do remember the judge talking directly to Big Mama.

"Due to the fact you're raising your grandson, I'm going to be lenient today and only fine you $225.00 plus damages and court cost. Also you'll be spending the next thirty days in the County Jail."

"Well you're sure a generous old son-of-a-bitch, aren't you," Big Mama blurted out so loud it seemed to echo off the courtroom walls.

I heard laughter behind us but was afraid to turn around and look. The judge's surprised look on his face immediately turned to anger. He slammed his gavel down and doubled the fine. Big Mama started to say something else when Papaw elbowed her in the side.

"Shut the hell up or we'll never get out of here," Papaw whispered. His voice was still loud enough for everyone to hear.

Two officers led Big Mama off cussing and kicking, as the judge ordered that I be placed in a temporary foster home.

◌◠◌

The people who ran the foster home were nice, and it was almost like having a normal family with a regular home. They even had a television, and a bicycle they let me ride around the block. I was just there over the weekend, as late Monday afternoon Papaw came to get me.

"Where's our pickup?" I asked Papaw, as we left the foster home and started walking down the street.

"I don't have the money to get the truck from the towing company so we'll just have to wait until I get my next check," he answered.

"Where are we going?" I asked, hoping it would be back to Bridge City.

"I don't know yet, but we'll have to hitchhike to get there. I think we'll just keep going north and look for a place along the way. How does that sound?" Papaw asked.

"Okay, I guess," but the truth was I was really unsure.

I was full of questions but afraid to ask. We walked across Texarkana and continued hiking north on Highway 71. It was hot, and I was getting hungry and thirsty. Papaw needed a drink too, but he didn't want water. He was always grouchy when he craved alcohol. My thoughts drifted back to Bridge City. I sure wished I was there.

After about an hour of hitchhiking we caught a ten mile ride to a turn off near the Red River Bridge. It was getting dark and no one was stopping, so Papaw and I camped near the end of the bridge. With no tent or sleeping bags, we just made ourselves as comfortable as the hard ground would allow. The night was beautiful with the temperature just right for sleeping. I lay on my back for a long time listening to Papaw snore and watching the stars. The crickets soon lulled me into a deep, peaceful sleep.

CHAPTER

TWENTY

The morning sun was already burning my face before Papaw was even awake. I was hungry and needed something to drink but was unsure if I should wake him up. Big Mama had warned me long before that if I woke him out of a dead sleep I may get hit or strangled. Often his dreams were from his Japanese prisoner of war days.

Using a long weed, I reached across from where I lay and began tickling his ear. When he started to wake up, I dropped the weed and pretended I was still sleeping. It didn't take him long to wake me, and soon we were back on the highway with our thumbs in the air.

We caught a ride within half an hour with the driver of a bread delivery truck. We had to sit on the steps as he made stops at stores along the way, but I was enjoying the ride. The best part was he supplied free donuts. He took us as far as DeQueen, Arkansas, before reaching the end of his route.

After walking across town, we caught a few more short rides. At last Papaw announced we had reached our final destination; the charming little town of Cove, Arkansas.

As we walked around town, everyone we met was friendly. I was relieved to see the school was small. I have no idea why we stopped in Cove, but this was the place Papaw chose for our home. Maybe he was just tired of hitchhiking, but then I was too.

The remains on an old abandoned sawmill at the edge of town became our temporary home. We spent the first night sleeping on a sawdust pile under a warm clear sky full of stars. A beautiful full moon made the buildings below us shine in the darkness like magic.

With the first touch of dew and light of the morning, we awoke and started the day fresh in our new town. Papaw shaved, using the rearview mirror on an abandoned car, and a can of water from a small creek. We spent the morning walking around town looking for a place to live.

Papaw talked someone into letting us rent a little house with the promise of paying when he got his Navy check. The house was one room. Not one bedroom – one room. It didn't have running water or even an inside bathroom, but it was better than sleeping outside.

Papaw didn't have the money to have the power turned on but at least it was a place to stay. I started school, even though I only had the clothes I was wearing. Most of our things were still in our pickup at the impound lot in Texarkana. Papaw dug a small hole in a little bog area behind the house where we could dip out a bucket of water each day to drink. The water just required filtering through a dish cloth to get the leaves and bugs out.

Papaw bummed, borrowed and stole everything we needed to get by. Our table and chairs came from the abandoned railroad station, but I doubt anyone cared, as Papaw and I carried then down the street in broad daylight. The local store owner let Papaw open a charge account for groceries until his next check came.

On the day that Papaw's check arrived, he paid his charge account in full at the store. He said he was going to hitch-hike to Texarkana to pick up our truck while I was at school. I was surprised when he came home later that day and had Big Mama with him. Not surprising was, they were both intoxicated. They talked about having to go back for court in a few months, and the fines that had to be paid. They will just never learn, I thought to myself.

We didn't live in the little house in Cove for long before Big Mama demanded that Papaw find another place to live. She was having a hard time accepting the occasional water snakes she would find out back in the outhouse.

"But Hon, there's not a lot of places to pick from," Papaw would moan. He knew he'd better find a place—the sooner the better.

After a lot of long drives, Papaw found a house out in the country that Big Mama was pleased with. The home was quite a few miles south of Cove and sat back off the highway about half a mile down a dirt lane. The paint was checked and peeling and the putty holding in the window panes was dried and falling out. Papaw and I started cutting down the high weeds that surrounded the place with a hand sickle. It didn't look like anyone had lived there in a hundred years. I'm not sure if Papaw paid rent or we just moved in.

There were grapes growing beside the dirt lane leading to

the house and an old corn field overgrown with weeds. The corn was too hard to eat, but it became my chore to grind it up with an old cast-iron-hand-crank-grinder. Big Mama would use the corn meal to make corn pies. It seemed like that's all we ever ate. When you're hungry you do what you have to, and eat what you have. Even so, I got sick of those dang corn pies each day. A chicken dinner would have been a pleasant change.

The house had running water until I was playing in the barn and stuck an old fashion soldering iron up inside the light socket. Sparks were flying everywhere as I pretended I was welding the side of a ship. Hundreds of sparks flew through the air and drifted to the floor each time I stuck the iron in the socket. The sparks reminded me of the ones I had often seen at the shipyard back in Orange, Texas. In just a few minutes the sparks stopped falling and we were without electricity from then on.

Fortunately for me, Big Mama and Papaw were both drinking when the electricity went out. If they had been sober, I would have been in deep trouble. When Big Mama was drunk, it was as if she looked for reasons to argue with Papaw. She blamed him for anything I did wrong.

"You know if you would show him more attention he probably would have had better things to do," she would say.

Across an overgrown field behind the house was a little creek with a sandy bottom. We soon had a well worn path from taking our baths there. Once in awhile I would see a snake while bathing but they were just water snakes and nothing to worry about. Big Mama and Papaw took baths at the same time so he could protect her. So they claimed.

With the electricity gone and the beer hot, Papaw and Big Mama started getting a little crankier with each passing day. In fact, they became down right unpleasant to be around and acted like they couldn't even stand each other or me for that matter. I spent as much time as possible exploring the hills and creeks around the house.

Papaw asked around and located a "bootlegger" just across the Oklahoma state line on Highway 4. Soon he was bringing home White Lightning in quart jars. Papaw handled his liquor better than Big Mama, but they both started drinking more and more each day. They were such good customer's; they got to know the "moon-shiner" on a personal basis. He began even trusting them to pay after Papaw's check came in each month. That meant they could stay drunk all the time. It also meant they wouldn't have any money left when their check came.

I went with Papaw a few times on his alcohol runs. He would pull up in the bootlegger's driveway, honk the horn and wait. A man would come out of the house and walk into the woods, then return shortly with a fruit jar full of moonshine liquor.

Papaw said the moon-shiner added snakeheads to the mash to give it bite, and he always took a big drink before driving back home just to test it. He said another way to test, was to pour a spoonful and light it on fire, and then dump it out. If it burned all the way to the floor it was good to drink. I wanted him to show me, but he said he already knew it was good from his taste test. Besides he didn't want to waste any. He always offered me a drink, knowing fully well I would turn it down.

"It'll kill that tapeworm you have in there," he said with a laugh as he pointed at my stomach.

E arly one afternoon Big Mama and Papaw got into a big argument because she said he was too damn lazy to fix the electricity in the house.

"I'm tired of going to bed when the sun goes down and bathing in the damn creek like some hillbilly," she cried.

He tried to explain to her that the wiring was burned up, and he didn't have the money to replace it, or the tools to do electrical work. She just wouldn't listen.

"If it was a damn Navy ship I bet you would fix it, you worthless bastard!" she yelled.

A few more comments like that and the fight was going strong. He said he was leaving but she refused to let him and blocked the front door. Papaw grew tired of listening to her and went to the bedroom to lay down for a nap.

Through all the arguments, I listened not so much to their words, but to the tone and anguish in their voices. I had witnessed many of their fights before and if it turned physical I didn't want to be there.

When Big Mama looked through the closet and came out with a hammer, I became nervous. Her eyes seemed glazed over as she staggered about, using the living room walls for support. I felt somewhat relieved when she went outside, still carrying the hammer.

Peeking out the window to see what she was going to do, I thought surely she isn't going to try and fix the electricity. I was surprised when she opened the hood to our pickup and started hitting engine parts.

She closed the hood and came back into the house like nothing was going on and then went into the bedroom. Soon the argument was going again and Papaw grabbed a few clothes and headed for the truck. Interestingly, she didn't try to stop him from leaving, but then again, she knew he wasn't going anywhere.

I watched from the front porch as Papaw tried to start the pickup, but all the engine would do was turn over. He raised the hood and called for me to try and start it again, while he looked under the hood. I had turned the engine over a few times when he started yelling to stop. He said the glass sediment bulb was broken, and gas was spraying all over the motor. He knew that Big Mama must have done this and was furious when he went back into the house.

It took a lot to make him angry, and I went back inside just to see what he was going to do to her. No punches were thrown but a lot of profanities were exchanged. Papaw grabbed some more clothes out of the closest and went out the back door, disappearing into the woods behind the house.

Big Mama was in a rage and began throwing things at the bedroom wall until she ran out of ammunition. Her ammunition was anything that was close enough for her to throw.

"Cliff, get you clothes packed," she yelled. "We're getting out of this damn hell hole and away from that worthless, no good bastard."

That wasn't the time to ask where we were going. I just did like she said and started packing my clothes in the smaller suitcase.

Big Mama was half packing, half destroying anything she didn't want to take with us. The cigar box that Papaw stored his World War II medals in flew across the room, spilling its contents. Big Mama saw my surprised look. "He probably stole the damn things. I'm sure the chicken shit bastard didn't do anything to earn them."

I knew how important the medals were to Papaw, so I picked up a few and stuck them in my pocket.

As we walked down the dirt lane toward the highway, the dirt felt hot against my bare feet. As much as I hated shoes, I wished I had worn them. Big Mama was cussing and calling Papaw names even though he wasn't in sight. I wondered where we were going, but I had been around her long enough not to ask questions.

When we reached the highway, Big Mama reached in her purse and handed me a $20 bill.

"What's this for?" I asked in surprise.

"Son, this is where we part company. You're old enough to make it on your own. You go that way—I'm going this way," she said, pointing toward the north.

I was stunned. I couldn't believe what Big Mama was telling me to do. I just stood there with my mouth open dumbfounded.

"Where should I go?" I asked her.

"Wherever you want to,—go back to Grandma's. Go to Colorado, go to hell. I don't care anymore."

She turned her back on me and started walking north on the shoulder of the highway toward Cove. I stood there for a few minutes in disbelief as she staggered across the highway and lifted her thumb toward passing cars.

I just wasn't sure what I should do. Did she really expect me to hitchhike 375 miles to Bridge City or all the way to Colorado? Should I just walk back to the house and see if Papaw would come back? If Big Mama saw me walking back home, I'd be in trouble for disobeying her.

After a few minutes, I took a deep breath and told myself *"I can do this."* I started walking south on the shoulder of the highway full of uncertainty and fear. A deep feeling of loneliness came over me. I looked back once in awhile, and could see Big Mama still walking the other way.

The last time I had sight of Big Mama, she had sat down in the ditch on top of her suitcase with her elbows on her knees and her face buried in her hands. She was wobbling from side to side like she was struggling to keep her balance and not fall off her suitcase. Normally I would have laughed, but the scene left a sick feeling in my stomach.

I walked for a few hours and tried hitchhiking when vehicles would pass, but no one slowed down. The hot pavement blistered my feet, and I longed for a drink of water. Relief came when I spotted a small bridge and a creek that flowed under the highway. Its water was clear and visible to the bottom. Working my way through the thick brush to the waters edge, I knelt down, cupping my hands into the cool water for a drink.

I sat there with my feet soaking in the stream for a long

while, not wanting to walk another step. A splash drew my attention to a water moccasin that dropped off a tree branch. Its thick black head stuck out of the water, while its body moved under the water's surface, propelling the snake across the creek toward me. Moving quickly, I made my way back up to the highway and continued walking south.

About three or four miles down the highway I came to a small country store. Remembering the $20 bill in my pocket, I went inside. The lady running the cash register gave me a funny look when I came in. I saw her glance out the window as if she expected a car to be waiting outside. Her eyes turned back on me with a puzzled look. I'm sure it appeared I came out of nowhere, but she never asked any questions.

I bought a bottle of chocolate soda pop, a peanut pattie and two ice cream bars. The clerk again looked mystified when I handed her my $20 bill. I crossed the highway to a large pine tree and sat down in the shade to enjoy my snack.

For about an hour I played in the dirt, and teased fire ants by plugging their holes with sticks.

On my second trip to the store, I bought a package of plastic toy soldiers from a rack near the counter, and a sack of cookies. I went back across the highway to the security of my shade tree and divided the soldiers equally, lining them up on two sides. I would sit on each side and throw dirt clods and see which side would win the war. It seemed like the American soldiers would always be the conqueror. I may have helped them out a little extra by throwing bigger clods. Reaching in my pocket, I awarded myself one of Papaw's medals for bravery.

On my third and fourth trip back to the store, I couldn't help but wonder if the lady would become suspicious enough to call the police. Maybe I even hoped she would. Surely she noticed I spent the afternoon under the tree. I wondered how many kids my age, ever came to the store unaccompanied with a $20.00 bill? Maybe she just liked the extra business and didn't care.

I asked myself a dozen times if I should just turn around and walk back home. Papaw was probably back home by now and wondering where we went. Maybe even Big Mama. She gave me orders to leave, so I guessed the best thing to do was just keep going. As drunk as she was, I suspect she probably went to jail for something.

My mind went through all of the possible options. If I could make it to Bridge City, Grandma would be glad to see me. I was sure she would let me stay, but there was still Uncle Rudy to worry about. Why did Big Mama even think I would want to go to Colorado? I guess she didn't know what it was like there.

I could just live in the woods the rest of my life, I reasoned. I wouldn't ever have to be around drunken people who fight all the time. So what if my Mom or no one else wanted me. Who needed them anyway? What an excellent idea! After all, Daniel Boone and Davy Crockett had both lived their lives in the wilderness. Tom Sawyer and Huckleberry Finn had dreamed of a life like this, but people tried to stop them. Nobody cared what I did anyway. I should be glad. It's settled, I thought to myself. The woods will be my new home.

Scouting out the area for the best place to build my shelter, I choose the big tree I had played under all day. Daniel Boone and Davy Crockett would have probably gone a little deeper into the forest to live, but this spot offered some advantages. Number one, the store was just across the highway, and that was a very big plus.

With darkness approaching, I began dragging dead tree limbs to my new camp site and leaning them up against the trunk of the tree. Breaking off limbs with leaves I soon had the outside layer of my makeshift lean-to covered with a roof. All that was left was to gather enough leaves to cover the ground and make a bed inside.

In just a few hours I had my new home finished. I laid down inside, very proud of my handiwork and smiled to myself. This has to be as nice as any Indian or mountain man could make. Looking at the leaves around me, I visualized how much nicer my hut would be if I had animal skins covering the floor. I would need to make a trap, but I didn't have any tools.

Glancing across the highway, I noticed the store had closed for the night. What was I thinking? Why didn't I buy a knife and matches while they were open? Tomorrow I would get all the things I needed to live here. Over time maybe I could build a log cabin. Another big advantage to living this way crossed my mind. No more school!

If I only had some matches to start a camp fire, I told myself. All the night sounds in the Arkansas woods had me worried. Be brave, I told myself. Davy Crockett wouldn't be afraid if he were here. But then Davy would probably have a gun and a knife.

A full chorus of chirping crickets sounded their tiny voices and grew louder and louder. After each noise in the darkness, it would become deathly silent. I strained my eyes after each sound, but I couldn't make out anything in the darkness. Probably just cottontails or maybe a possum, I tried to convince myself.

I was becoming jumpy with each new sound coming ever closer to my shelter. If I just had my BB gun, I wouldn't be so afraid. Even a flashlight would be great.

A loud scream like someone in distress just outside my shelter broke my train of thought, and brought me to a sitting position. It was followed by evil laughter and what sounded like a woman's voice yelling. I almost needed some clean underwear. A witch was the first thing that entered my mind. I could almost see her face!

I knocked the wall down on my shelter and ran toward the highway looking back over my shoulder. As I ran full speed, I heard a noise above me and looked up to see the wings of a large owl racing me out of the woods. The owl probably had no idea I was camped under the bushes at the base of the tree. It was probably as terrified as I was. Those Arkansas woods can be scary at night, especially for a 9 year old boy. My living in the woods ordeal was over, and I decided it was time to try hitchhiking again.

My heart had just started to slow down to a normal beat when a propane truck came around the curve and lit me up with its bright lights. The truck slowed down as it passed me, and then the brake lights came on as it pulled to the side of the road. It worked—I had never hitchhiked alone before but I had a ride. I ran through the darkness as the dust settled and nervously climbed up the steps to the passenger door. The tall lanky driver reached across the seat and opened the door.

"Where you headed?" he asked as he tried to peel the foil off a stick of gum.

"I'm going to my Grandma's in Bridge City, Texas," I answered nervously.

"Well, climb on in here boy. Are you running away from home?" he asked inquisitively.

"No sir, my Big Mama and Papaw had a big fight. She gave me some money and told me to go to Texas to my Grandma's."

"No kidding! I drove by several times today and noticed you hanging out over by the trees all afternoon. How old are you?" he asked, as he glanced in my direction.

"I'll be turning ten in September," I answered.

He blew a bubble and let it pop, then turned and looked at me. "Your Big Mama, huh? That's pretty strange. You sure you're not running away? You look awful young to be out here all by yourself."

"No sir, I'm not lying."

He would probably call the police, but I really didn't care. Maybe that's what needed to happen. At this point in my life, I needed someone to make decisions for me. A sign said Texarkana, 65 miles. Maybe I should just go back to the foster home. I'm sure they would let me stay there. My thoughts were broken by the driver's voice. "You'll never catch a ride here," he said. "I'll take you to the intersection where another highway comes in, and I'm sure you'll have more traffic there."

I had no idea where I was when he finally pulled over and

stopped. Somewhat frightened and apprehensive, I thanked him for the ride and climbed out of the truck into the darkness. Standing alone at the lonely intersection, I watched as his tail-lights disappeared into the night. I was wishing I had just gone wherever he was going.

Soon I was sticking my thumb in the air as cars zoomed by without slowing down. As each car raced passed, I raised my thumb in the air, begging for a ride. The headlights of another speeding car went to high beam as it sped by. I blinked and closed my eyes momentarily, allowing my eyes to re-adjust to the darkness and took in a deep breath of exhaust filled air.

It's all right, I reminded myself over and over. Everything will be fine.

My luck improved about an hour later when a late model car went by but suddenly stopped and backed up. The middle aged man driving was dressed in a suit and appeared nice but talked like a Yankee. The man was full of questions. I told him all about Big Mama and Papaw and why I was hitchhiking. He, too, asked me how old I was and seemed shocked when I told him.

"I think you're awful young to be out here on the highway, especially at night. Where are you headed to?"

"I'm going to Bridge City, Texas to live with my Grandma," I answered with as much confidence as possible.

He seemed to be studying my face like he didn't believe me. After a long silence he answered; "What a coincidence. You're in luck because I'm going to the very same town you are."

I felt like my guardian angel was truly watching over me and breathed a sigh of relief. When he offered to buy me supper I turned him down, as I didn't feel the best from all the junk food I had eaten all afternoon. As the miles passed by, I stared out the windshield into the darkness. Won't Grandma be surprised when I show up in Bridge City? My thoughts went back over all the things that had happened that day; Big Mama and Papaw fighting and my camping in the woods, the hoot owl that almost caused me to soil my pants. It had truly been a day I wouldn't forget.

The tires on his car hummed softly against the pavement as the headlights cut through the darkness. Soon the soft music playing on the radio lulled me into a deep sleep.

When the car stopped for a traffic light, the sudden quietness woke me. Looking around I noticed we were in a city, and rubbed my eyes from the glare of the street lights.

"Where are we?"

"Texarkana," the man replied. He didn't say anything else as we drove along in silence. I could tell something was wrong.

I wasn't surprised when he pulled up in front of a large building with police cars parked outside. I recognized the building from the last time I was here with Big Mama and Papaw.

"I have a good friend up here I want you to meet," he said.

I followed him into the building wondering what the police were going to do with me. Maybe they would just take me back to Big Mama, I reasoned. Maybe it would be different if the police took me back. It wouldn't be like I was disobeying her orders and going back on my own. I wondered if the police could just give me a ride to Bridge City. If they gave me a choice, that's where I would go.

We walked down the hallway in silence. I'm sure he was embarrassed for lying to me, but it didn't matter. He told me he was going to Bridge City too, and now here we were in the police station.

The man knocked on one of the office doors and a gruff voice yelled, "Come in." I didn't pay much attention to their conversation, as I was intrigued by the wanted posters hanging on the walls. The police calls were blasting on the radio. I think I'll become a police officer when I grow up, I thought to myself, as I surveyed my surroundings.

"Son, come over here and have a seat. I understand my friend here picked you up hitchhiking outside of DeQueen.

"Yes sir," I answered.

"Why don't we start with your name," the officer behind the desk asked.

"Cliff Johnson," I answered, still scanning my surroundings.

"How old are you son?"

"I'll be ten years old in September," I answered with pride.

"Okay Cliff, we're off to a good start. What are your parent's names?"

"I think my Mom's name is Patsy, but I don't know my dad's name. I don't know where they live. I think my mom's in prison somewhere. Maybe Kansas or Texas, I'm not sure."

"What's she in prison for?"

"Writing hot checks, I guess. I'm not really sure."

"You don't even know your dad's name? Do you expect me to believe that?"

I just shrugged my shoulders. The officer frowned at me like I was lying.

"Now this is really important, so you think hard about it before you answer. What's your address?"

"I really don't know for sure, because we just moved to Arkansas."

The frown on his face said he didn't believe me.

I told him the whole story in detail about Big Mama and Papaw's fight and why I was hitchhiking, but the officer behind the desk just shook his head and frowned.

"You're lying to me, and I don't appreciate that. I know you ran away and I want some honest answers."

"I already told you, I didn't run away! I'm telling you the truth," I answered, struggling to hold back the tears that were building inside.

"Okay, lets try this another way. What's your Grandma and Grandpa's name, and where do they live?"

"Well, my Grandma's name is Big Mama, and my Grandpa's name is Papaw. I already told you I don't know their address. My Great Grandmother lives in Bridge City and that's where I was going," I replied.

That answer produced a look from hell as the officer tapped his pen on his note pad and stared me down with his cold, dark eyes.

"What's the phone number for your grandma in Bridge City?"

"She doesn't have a phone."

"Then what's your Big Mama's phone number?"

"She doesn't have a phone either," I answered, knowing he wouldn't believe me. I was growing tired of all the questions.

The officer stood up and slammed his notebook down on his

desk. "How convenient, no one has a phone. Well let me tell you something, Cliff, or whatever your real name is. You better start giving me some straight answers right now, or you're going to find yourself locked up for a long time. Is that what you want?"

"No sir, but I'm telling you the truth. I don't know the address where we live. I just know it's down a lane off the highway somewhere between Cove and DeQueen. I could show you if you want to drive me back there."

He must have asked me questions for an hour, but I honestly didn't have the answers he wanted. Soon he was back to asking the same questions over again.

"Let's talk about your dad. What's his name and where does he live?"

"I told you. I don't know who my dad is or where he lives. I have a step-dad named Morris. Sometimes he lives in Burlington, Colorado." The expression on his face told me he liked that answer better than those I gave about Big Mama.

His next question was; what does Morris do for a living.

"I think he's a fire eater with the carnival," I answered.

That reply brought a chuckle from the man who gave me the ride, and some of the other officers that were watching. The officer asking the questions pushed a button on his phone without looking up. There was disgust written all over his face.

"Get him out of here!" he yelled into the speaker phone.

I think it was that answer that got me locked up. I knew I shouldn't have told the officer that Morris was a fire eater, but it just came out. One of those things you wish you could take back but it was too late. It was said and there was no changing it.

Morris bragged that he and my Mom had traveled with a carnival. If he was drinking, his ability to blow a flame of fire out of his mouth over the top of his cigarette lighter always came up. I never witnessed him do it, but he explained how he could fill his mouth with rubbing alcohol and blow a flame without getting burned. It sounded possible. I honestly thought maybe that's what he did on the carnival. I thought it would sound better than having to tell the officer I didn't know.

A uniformed officer placed me in the back seat of his patrol car and drove to a residential area of town. I'm not sure if you would call the place where he took me a detention center, but it was certainly a step beyond the foster home I had been in before. It was just an older house, but with one difference. Wire mesh covered the window of the bedroom.

I spent my days and nights locked in the room with nothing to do but look out the window and wish I was anyplace else. There was no bathroom in the room, so if I had to go, it meant knocking on the door and being escorted by a big fat lady who really hated her job.

Being considered an uncooperative runaway had some definite disadvantages. For one thing, I didn't have the privileges the other boys had. An older boy I shared the room with, named Mike, worked somewhere and only had to stay locked up at night. He noticed me looking at him my first night there.

"What are you looking at punk?" he said in a low snarl.

"Nothing," I said, and turned my head to avoid eye contact

with him. He sensed my weakness and pushed his intimidation a step higher.

"Are you saying I'm nothing? Get over here right now. What are you in here for?" he asked. "Probably sniffing little girls tricycle seats," one of the other boys laughed.

I could tell them I knew how to box and they better just leave me alone, but I didn't think they would be impressed. Besides, the last fight I had been in was the one Big Mama arranged when we lived in Deweyville, and I lost.

"Do you have any money?" Mike asked, as he twisted the front of my shirt in a knot, and pushed me against the wall.

I wasn't sure how much I had left from the $20.00 bill that Big Mama gave me, but I told him I had some. I was hoping he wouldn't search me and find Papaw's medals.

"How much you got?" one of the boys asked as they both huddled around me.

As I pulled the money from my pocket, Mike jerked it from my hands. Grinning, he grabbed me by the throat and pushed me against the wall.

"You want me to have this because we're friends don't you?" he asked with a testy look.

Too afraid to answer, all I could do was nod my head yes.

"If you tell . . ." Mike doubled up his fist and rubbed my chin with his knuckles, "I'll kill you."

I hated this place. There was nothing to do day after day but sit on the bed and throw spit wads at cockroaches. If I didn't wait until I heard a commercial on television for my bathroom visits, the lady running the place would be very irritated at my interruption. More than once, she threw a hissy-fit when she missed part of her soap opera. God forbid if I had to go to the bathroom during the night.

The weeks crawled slowly by, and I hated being there more with each passing day. No one seemed to know what was going to happen to me, and asking questions didn't seem to help. I had the helpless feeling that no one even knew I was there; even the police had probably forgotten about me.

"I'm only 9 years old. Will I have to stay locked up until I'm 18?" I asked myself.

❦

One afternoon during a television commercial, I asked the warden if she could call someone and ask when I was going to be released.

"Absolutely not, when its time for you to be released I'll let you know," she answered with a sour scowl.

"Absolutely not," I mumbled, making an ugly face and repeating what she said when her head was turned. I was really starting to dislike them damn Yankees. Her answer and attitude was all it took—the decision was made. I was busting out!

My constant thought was how to escape. I knew the Red River was close to Texarkana, and that it flowed south. I had seen the Red River Bridge in Shreveport and also in Alexandria, Louisiana. If I could make it to the river I would be home free. Most bridges always have boats tied up under them. If I found one, I could float all the way to New Orleans or even the Gulf of Mexico.

Stealing is wrong I thought to myself, but hey—I'm locked up already. They're already treating me like a criminal. What would they do if they caught me? Probably just bring me back to this awful place. It looked like I was going to be here all my life anyway if I didn't do something. The hard part would be getting away from this hell hole and Texarkana without the police catching me.

I fell into a deep sleep and dreamed about Tom Sawyer, Huckleberry Finn and their river trip. I could sure relate to them and their experiences. Huck knew what it was like to grow up on the wrong side of the river, and not have anyone who wanted him. Too bad I didn't have Tom for a partner.

I decided that's it. No more putting it off. It was time to put my plan into action. No more looking out the window and wishing I was somewhere else.

I knocked on the bedroom door in the middle of the afternoon and announced I really needed to go to the bathroom. She was right in the middle of watching *Search For Tomorrow* on television and acted really annoyed that I was disturbing her. After unlocking my door, she went right back to her ironing board and was almost in a hypnotic state. All her concentration was on the television.

Everything was going just like I planned. She didn't even notice me quietly come out of the bathroom without flushing and walk quietly to the front door.

I held my breath as I pushed out on the screen door, but it didn't budge. The dang thing was latched. Quickly I struggled with the latch trying to pull it free, but it was stuck.

"What in the hell are you doing?" the lady yelled, as she waddled toward me like a mad grizzly bear ready to pounce on its prey.

"I just want to go outside and sit on the porch," I replied.

"You know good and well you're not allowed to do that."

"It's not like I'm trying to run away. I just want out of that room and need some fresh air. Please—just let me go outside for a few minutes," I pleaded.

She wouldn't let me outside, but she must have felt somewhat sorry for me, because I didn't have to go back to the room. All I could do was sit and watch soap operas and Procter and Gamble commercials with her. That was better than nothing, but it was almost border-line cruel and unusual punishment.

✦

About a month had passed when Big Mama showed up in a taxi. I breathed a sigh of relief. How she found me, I have no idea, but I'm guessing it took so long because they had to wait for their next month's Navy check to come in. I think she went along with the story that I was a runaway to keep herself out of trouble. She must have made the proper arrangements for my release because the lady watching me looked over hepaperwork and told me I was free to go.

Big Mama was sober, the first time I had seen her that way in a long time. As we rode in the taxi to the bus station, she asked how much money she had given me the day I left home. When I told her $20.00 she suddenly seemed happy.

"How much do you have left?" Big Mama asked, her eyes dancing with excitement.

"None—one of the boys I was locked up with took it away from me. He said he would kill me if I told anyone, but I still have Papaw's medals."

Big Mama's expression changed to one of deep disappointment. Her hands were shaking badly, and I could tell she needed a drink. Most likely, she had been looking forward to a drink all day. She was very grumpy on the bus ride back home, and snapped at me to never do this again.

"But Big Mama, you're the one who packed my clothes and said to go to Texas," I reminded her.

I could see a tear form in the corner of her eye, but I couldn't tell if it was because she was sorry for what she did or she was just craving more alcohol.

As we crossed the bridge over the Red River, I looked down at the water and thought to myself: I was almost here. I wonder what it would have been like if I had made it?

Big Mama had to go back to Texarkana for court on her driving while intoxicated charge for running over the Coca-Cola Cop. She didn't have the money for the fine she was suppose to pay and knew she would probably be going to jail. Papaw had found a replacement sediment bulb for our pickup that Big Mama had broken, and he spent the day getting it running again. He planned to drive Big Mama to Texarkana while I was in school.

The next morning I rushed to get ready to catch the school bus, as Big Mama prepared to spend some time in jail.

"Cliff, you have plenty of clean clothes to last you in this box, so try not to get dirty. There's food in the cupboard and don't wander off too far after school. Papaw has enough on his mind without having to worry about you."

Big Mama gave out a few more orders, and I wished her luck as I went out the door and headed to school. I had a hard time concentrating all day; my mind was on Big Mama and what was going on in the court room. I wondered if she would get mad and call the judge names again.

When I came home from school, no one was home. Most kids would probably be upset if their parents went to jail, but it really didn't bother me that much. By now it had happened enough I was getting use to it, and I just went with the flow, like a muddy river. The hours slowly passed by and I wondered if Papaw had gone to jail too.

Hunger has a way of bringing on worry, and I watched the hour hand on the alarm clock move at the pace of a snail. With no other sounds in the room, the clock's ticking got on my nerves. After checking the cupboard I found enough food to last a few days; a box of oatmeal, peanut butter, grits, cane syrup, a bottle of tomato catsup and half a loaf of bread. I fixed myself another catsup sandwich and sat down in the chair studying the Texaco road map. I had looked at that old map so many times that I had the route to Bridge City almost memorized. Knowing my way around the country might be just as important someday as hunting and fishing skills. You just never know when you may need to find your way home. It does get confusing if you don't know where home is.

Grandma had often read Scriptures from the Bible to me. I sat there watching for Papaw and thought of the words she had me memorize: "Consider the ravens: they do not sow or reap, they have no storeroom or barn, yet God feeds them. And how much more valuable are you than birds?"

I knelt down and had a serious talk with the Lord.

"Jesus, I know I wanted to come to Arkansas with Big Mama and Papaw, but I'm really starting to not like it here. I know Grandma is getting too old to take care of me, but Jesus, I think I'd be better off living with her in Bridge City. So if you could make that happen, I would appreciate it. Amen."

I was sound asleep when Papaw returned home during the night without Big Mama. He was falling down drunk, and walked around the house cussing and kicking things out of his way. I wanted to ask if Big Mama went back to jail, but already knew the answer and felt it was better not to ask.

To my surprise, he told me to pack my things. He said he was taking me back to Bridge City. Wow, that's amazing I thought, smiling to myself. I just prayed for that and now, almost like magic, I'm going back to Bridge City. God sure answers prayers fast!

For some reason Papaw acted mean and cold toward me, snapping at my questions. It was really out of character for him to act this way, but he seemed to be more intoxicated than usual. Ever since he started drinking bootleg whiskey, he had become meaner.

We loaded the pickup with what few things I had and headed for Bridge City in the middle of the night. Papaw never drove anywhere after dark. God must have really gotten his attention for us to be leaving without waiting until morning.

As we traveled down the highway in silence, a man hitchhiking appeared in our headlights. Papaw swerved to miss him. The pickup fishtailed, its tires sliding sideways on the asphalt, and the pickup leaning as if it would turn over. At last we came to rest in the weeds beside the highway.

The man who was hitchhiking ran up excited and asked if we were okay. I thought of one of Grandma's famous warnings: You should always wear clean underwear because you just never know when you may be in an accident. Strange how that thought came to mind.

"Can you drive?" Papaw asked the man.

"Sure," he answered, with a surprised look on his face. The hitchhiker drove us to Texarkana, where he woke up Papaw and thanked him for the ride. It seemed like Texarkana was always the center hub for traveling anywhere. Almost like a magical gate that had to be passed through for any destination.

I was hoping Papaw would want to stay there for the night, but I couldn't be that lucky. I wondered if we were even going the right direction, but I sure wasn't going to ask.

In his drunken condition Papaw kept running off the road onto the shoulder. He wouldn't wake up when I called his name. I would have to physically reach over and shake him. Each time he would cuss and jerk the steering wheel, bringing the truck back on the road.

Soon we were off the highway and headed for the ditch again. In a panic, I grabbed Papaw's arm and called him.

"Would you just shut the hell up? You're not driving the son-of-a-bitch," he yelled, jerking his arm away from me.

I bet he wouldn't talk that way if Big Mama was here to put him in his place, I thought. After that I was afraid to say anything. He had never struck me before, but he seemed angry enough that I didn't want to take a chance and make this his first time. I decided that if he went to sleep again, I'd just teach him a lesson and not wake him. I didn't care if he did wreck his stupid truck.

Just a few more miles down the highway, it happened again. Slowly, the pickup drifted off on the shoulder. This time we were headed straight for a large concrete culvert. I glanced at the speedometer: Forty-five miles per hour. I'll teach him not to yell at me.

Putting my feet against the dash, I braced myself for the impending crash. We continued toward the culvert, seeming to pick up speed before reaching it.

The wreck was much worse than I expected. In a split second, my feet shot downward toward the floorboard, and the impact drove my head through the windshield. We came to a sudden stop with my knees against the dash. The top half my body was outside on the hood, face down. Broken glass flickered on the hood like stars, as the lights from passing cars went by without stopping.

We were so far off the highway no one even noticed us. Only the crumpled hood of the car protected me from the scalding steam that was spraying and hissing underneath my head.

My head throbbed. I rubbed the lump on my head that seemed to be growing in size, and checked my fingers for blood. I just couldn't see anything in the darkness. It didn't feel like it was bleeding, even though I had a lot of glass in my hair. Papaw was having trouble breathing, and was holding his side complaining that he broke his ribs, as he wiped his bloody nose.

That will teach him to yell at me, I thought to myself. Should I rub it in and say, I tried to tell you? No—it probably wouldn't be a good idea.

Papaw told me to walk over to one of the houses where the porch lights had just came on, and see if someone would call a wrecker to pull us out of the ditch. I told Papaw I didn't think it would help because the front of our truck was caved in, and was smoking badly.

"Just go ask um, damn it!" he yelled, holding his side in pain and groaning.

As I walked toward the houses I thought if God had arranged this middle of the night trip then he also protected me from being hurt in the wreck. Papaw better be careful yelling at me because Jesus was the one in control here, and I was one of his children. He apparently didn't know who he was messing with.

Of the three houses with porch lights, one didn't have dogs so I chose that one. A lady answered the door and seemed very frightened.

"My goodness, your just a boy. Come on inside," she said and opened the door. "Are you okay?" Her kids gathered around me with their mouths open and gawking.

"Yes Ma'am, I'm okay. I just have a bump on my head where I went through the windshield."

She checked the bump closer and then combed glass out of my hair. "I think you should see a doctor," she said with a worried look, as she gently felt the knot which had grown in size.

"I'll be fine," I assured her. "It's just sore, and I have a little headache. My Papaw is bleeding from his nose and said his ribs are broken. He wants to know if you'll call us a wrecker," I asked embarrassed, knowing a tow truck couldn't do anything to help us.

"I called the police when I heard the crash. I'm sure they'll get someone out to help him. Do you want to just wait here until they come?"

"No Ma'am, I better go back out and make sure he's okay, and let him know help's on the way."

I knew what would happen when the police got there, but I sure wasn't going to tell Papaw. He would really be mad if he knew the police were coming instead of a wrecker.

Papaw was still sitting in the pickup holding on to what was left of the steering wheel when I went back to the pickup.

"Do they have help coming," he asked?

"Yes Sir, I'm sure they will be here anytime," I answered, keeping exactly who was coming a secret.

He kept complaining about the pain in his ribs, but at least his nose bleed had slowed down.

Half an hour had passed and Papaw grew impatient. He decided we should walk back down the highway toward Texarkana and find another tow truck. Each step he took seemed to cause him pain, and he cursed with each breath.

We hadn't walked too far when a police car pulled up behind us. The officer asked if we were okay as he looked us over with his flashlight. The officer placed Papaw in the back and let me ride in the front seat with him.

Making a U-turn, the police officer drove back to our wrecked truck and lit it up with his spotlight. Papaw and I waited in the patrol car as the officer looked over the damage. Papaw mumbled something about what he was going to charge to pull us out, and I fought back a laugh.

When the officer returned to the patrol car he checked my head and said I was lucky I wasn't killed. He just couldn't believe that I wasn't even injured. "You know God was really looking out for you tonight?" he said, as he examined my head.

I nodded my head in agreement and thought to myself; Yes, He was.

I asked the officer a hundred questions as we continued down the highway. "What does this switch do? How do you make your cop lights come on? Can you turn the siren on?" I'm sure I must have driven him nuts, but he was more than willing to answer all my questions. Once in awhile Papaw would mumble something and cuss from the back seat. My mind was made up. I wanted to be a cop when I grow up.

We must have been 15 or 20 miles from Texarkana. The officer spotlighted a few businesses and talked on his radio to other officers as we traveled down the highway.

It wasn't until after we arrived in Texarkana, and the officer was taking Papaw out of the back seat that Papaw noticed he wasn't riding in a wrecker.

"Why you're a goddamn cop!"

The officer couldn't help but laugh. "Why yes I am, and you're obviously very drunk." We had been riding with the officer all this time in a marked patrol car, and Papaw was too intoxicated to have even noticed it.

There was no doubt in my mind that he was going to jail for a long time. Again I couldn't help but wonder what were they going to do with me?

✦

It was like a home coming when I went back to the same foster home where I had stayed before. I was thankful it wasn't the juvenile detention center again. The lady who ran the home acted like she was really glad to see me. The police advised her of my injury and to watch me for awhile before I went to sleep. I knew I would be okay.

It seemed strange that Big Mama and Papaw were both in jail at the same time, in the same city, but I doubt they were able to see each other. Most likely, Big Mama didn't even know Papaw had been arrested, or that I was in a foster home. With a safe place to stay and three delicious meals a day, why should I worry about them? I guess it's kind of selfish, but I was more concerned about my future.

Big Mama and Papaw must have received lengthy sentences, as it had been almost three months and I hadn't heard from them. The lady who ran the home said I needed to be placed somewhere permanently, because I had been in foster care longer than was allowed. I wondered if I would be placed for adoption somewhere. It really didn't matter to me; nothing I could do would change the situation anyway. Once in awhile my thoughts would drift off to the Red River and the adventures that waited there, but I had no reason to run. Maybe I would be better off being adopted by someone who wanted me. All I could do was just wait and see what happened. The river would always be there waiting if things didn't work out.

One afternoon, I was playing games in my room with some of the other kids who lived in the home. I didn't pay much attention to the knock on the door. People came and went all the time, so it wasn't unusual.

"Cliff, please come in here," the lady who ran the home called. I went to the living room where a group of people were standing, but I avoided eye contact. Probably the people from

the state, and they're going to place me somewhere else, I surmised. I wasn't sure how I should act.

"Cliff, do you know this man?" one of the ladies asked.

"No ma'am," I answered, embarrassed to look him in the
face.

"It's your Uncle Mel. Don't you recognize him?"

I looked up in disbelief. I'd never seen him dressed in a suit.
When he grinned, I knew it was really him. Uncle Mel always
wore cowboy boots and a white cowboy hat with dirt on the
brim. He looked out of place dressed in a suit.

Uncle Mel spoke first. "Cliff, would you like to come live
with me and your Aunt Verna?"

I could feel my face glow with pride. Here at last was someone who really wanted me. Uncle Mel signed all the required
paper work, and helped me load my things. I told my friends
and my temporary family at the foster home goodbye, knowing
I would never see them again.

Uncle Mel never talked a lot, but he made conversation as he
drove. "Verna stayed home to get your room ready. She's been
painting and putting up wall paper the last few days. We're living in Pasadena, Texas in a small apartment, but I think you're
going to like it."

I knew I would, but the thought of a new school and living
in a city loomed in the back of my mind like a bad dream.

I watched Uncle Mel drive as the sun dropped below the
horizon. His face was weathered by the sun and wind, with
deep lines around his eyes. I could see the affects of hard physical labor written all over him. To me, he was what you would

call a real cowboy's cowboy, a true defender of the underdogs of the world and young boys needing help.

Even though Verna and Uncle Mel had rescued me from the foster home, I felt somewhat out of place there. They were still newlyweds, and I couldn't help but wonder if they felt sorry for me or really did want me living with them. They probably wanted to have their own children. Why would they want a boy that was as old as me? I wondered why I wasn't taken back to Grandma's in Bridge City, but then I remembered—Uncle Rudy of course. That explained it all.

My social skills were completely lacking, and I dreaded the thought of going to another new school. There were other kids in the neighborhood, but I avoided them, preferring to just ride the bike that Uncle Mel had bought me. I had played by myself for so long that I just wasn't comfortable around other kids.

Maybe I was worried they would ask questions I didn't want to answer. My low self-esteem had produced an invisible roadblock that I carried deep inside me. It felt so strong at times that I was afraid others could see it.

CHAPTER

TWENTY-THREE

Uncle Mel, Verna and I were watching television when a knock came on the door. The only people who ever knocked were our downstairs neighbor complaining about my stomping around. Verna jumped up to answer the door, ready to fight. She knew I had been sitting on the couch for an hour so there was no reason for them to complain.

To our surprise it was my Mom, Morris and Rocky. Verna almost tripped on her tongue. "I'm uh—surprised to see you. How—I mean, when did you get out?" Verna asked.

"About a week ago, and it would be better if you didn't ask a lot of questions." Mom answered. "You boys go in the other room and play. We need to have a private conversation."

I closed the door behind me as Rocky explored my room. I had my head to the door listening to ever word in the living room.

"Verna, I'm his mother and he belongs with me."

"But he's been moved around so often, he's behind in school. I talked to his teacher the other day, and she said he's just now starting to improve. He has friends here. It's not fair to drag him off again. If you escaped, the police will be looking for you. That's no way to raise your boys; always on the run and looking over your shoulder," Verna cried.

"I don't care what you think!" Mom shouted. "He's going

with us, and that's final."

Mom's visit was short. She had me pack my things in the car, and give Verna and Uncle Mel a goodbye hug, all within twenty minutes

"What about my bike?" I asked, as I made my last trip down the stairs.

"We don't have room for it son, but I promise I'll get you another one when we get settled," Mom assured me.

"I'll keep it for you, Cliff." Uncle Mel assured me.

After tearful hugs and good-byes, Mel told me to always remember that I had a home with them if I ever needed one.

It wasn't that I disliked living with Aunt Verna and Uncle Mel, but it just seemed right to be with my Mom and little brother. The future was full of promises, though I didn't know where we were going other than north.

I listened to Mom and Morris argue for hours about where were going to live. Mom wanted to live in Fort Worth, while Morris thought Seminole, Oklahoma offered a better chance for finding work. "The oil fields are crying for experienced roughnecks," Morris argued. I fell asleep, not really caring where we went. I just wanted out of the car.

❧

The house we moved into in Seminole, Oklahoma is what Mom called typical oilfield. The school was large and intimidating. I hadn't even learned my way around before we were packed and moving again.

This time we didn't move as far. Mom got her wish, but still argued that we should have moved to Fort Worth to begin with. Mom had an old girlfriend named Corinne that lived there. Mom thought Corinne could help us get established without drawing a lot of attention. I wasn't sure what she meant by, "help us get established." It started making sense when Mom rented a house and Corinne put all the utilities in her name.

Only a few more months of school remained. I was already so far behind that Mom said I could just start my summer vacation early if I wanted to. Besides that, Morris was worried that having my school records transferred might lead the police to our location. Mom said I had changed schools so often, they probably couldn't even find my records.

Morris found a job working in a gas station but hated it. Each night he came home complaining about the asshole he worked for, and the stupid customers he had to deal with each day.

When summer came, Mom thought I was old enough to help earn an income and found me a job selling ice cream in downtown Fort Worth. Pushing a vendor's cart all over town was fun at first, (maybe the first two hours) but when the heat of the mid-afternoon sun hit, I was eating ice cream faster than I was selling it. As I pushed my cart along the streets, I could smell the hot asphalt vapors as it drifted up from the pavement.

I learned real fast that the good downtown street corner locations were taken by older established vendors. In no uncertain terms I was told to move on more than once. It seemed like no matter where I went, my presence was met with rejection.

As I pushed my cart passed what looked like a school, about 50 kids rushed up to the fence wanting ice cream. Must be some kind of summer school, I thought. Now, this is the way to sell ice cream.

A lady came out of the building and walked up to where I stood. Once again I received a butt chewing. She went on to tell me how mean and cruel I was to come in front of an orphanage and tease all the children with my ice cream. How was I to know it was an orphanage? I felt like an old stray dog must feel as it gets chased out of yards all over town with other dogs nipping at its heels.

Mid-afternoon my luck changed when I discovered the Trinity River flows through Fort Worth. I pushed my ice cream cart down a slight grade and leaned back against the trunk of a tree near the waters edge. Shielded from the blistering sun, I spent hours watching the river flow by, daydreaming and eating ice cream. It was just too hot to move.

At the end of the day, the business manager tallied up how much ice cream I had sold and then counted the money I turned in. With a puzzled look on his face, he re-counted it again, just to make sure he hadn't made a mistake. Unfortunately, I owed them. My ice cream selling career came to an abrupt halt. My crotch was rubbed raw from pushing that cart all over town, and I doubt I could have lasted another day anyway. I walked bow-legged for the next three days, just to keep my jeans from rubbing.

Corinne was a major Tupperware dealer, and even won a free car for her high sales volume. She convinced Mom to go into the home party business too. Mom seemed to be making a lot of money selling Tupperware, and we were starting to look like your normal everyday family. Sometimes my hopes and dreams overrode the past hurts and disappointments. Being a normal family was what I wanted, but I still couldn't help but worry. How can anything be close to normal when the FBI may show up at anytime and arrest your mom?

I joined the Boy Scouts but felt like I knew more about the outdoors than those city kids ever would. I wondered how many of them had ever caught poisonous snakes or ate turtle soup. Had they ever caught crabs with a string or been up to their waist in quicksand, or face-to-face with an alligator? I don't think so. I felt like a country boy hanging out with a bunch of sissy city slickers.

I did agree to go to scout camp and quickly found a group of boys to hang out with who seemed to be more like me—the wrong side of the river type. It made my being there easier, but the potential of getting into trouble was greater. I'm sure there was an abundance of things to learn, but I was in the self-destruction mode and not open to new ideas.

The scoutmaster just didn't measure up to my image of a real scout leader. He was nothing like John Wayne or some of the other male figures I was starting to admire. He tried to teach me how to use a compass but as far as I was concerned there were only three directions that mattered; up the river, down the river and across the river.

With the permission of our scout leader, we set up our tent across the highway from the rest of the group. After all, we were different and wanted our independence. There was definitely a power struggle underway. When the other scouts were sound asleep, we raided their camp for food and went skinny dipping in the lake. We stayed out half the night and slept in late in the morning skipping breakfast. Not your typical Boy Scouts of America by any means.

While walking back to our tent after an evening of skinny dipping in the lake, a group of cars came up behind us and started blowing their horns. Still naked, we walked in the lane of traffic to avoid the stickers on the side of the highway. All the honking drew the Scoutmaster's interest long enough for him to look out of his tent and see our bare butts shining in the car's headlights. The police showed up a short time later; our scouting days were over. Our Scoutmaster cut the trip short and took us all home three days early. That's pretty pathetic when you get kicked out of the Boy Scouts. My downward spiral was gaining momentum.

I guess it's just as well that we moved before I started school in Fort Worth. Mom started writing bad checks again, flooding Fort Worth with worthless paper before we left town. Morris was drinking, and Rocky and I were fighting over space in the back seat. We were on the road again, final destination: Unknown.

We went to Oklahoma City and Tulsa, spending a day in each city and then a few hours in Joplin, Missouri, as Mom continued her check writing marathon. She complained that Joplin was too damn close to Lansing, Kansas, home to the women's prison. The nearness made her nervous, and Morris took advantage of that.

"Would you like to go to Kansas City? They have a lot of businesses there you could hit," Morris joked. "Maybe even drive through Lansing and see if they fixed the whole in the fence yet."

"Not only no—but hell no!" she laughed as she stuck her tongue out at him. Though we were cooped up in the car or motel rooms, I was enjoying being a family.

With even more checks cashed in Jefferson City and Columbia, Morris drove on to St. Louis. We spent the night there, and moved to Hannibal, Missouri. Mom said that as long as you have checks, you have money, and she wasn't going to stop writing until she ran out.

Mom decided it was time for a day off. We blended in like all the other tourists in the boyhood home of Mark Twain. Hannibal was an enjoyable change of pace as well as an opportunity to walk the streets where the "Adventures of Tom Sawyer" had taken place. At the edge of town I could see the mighty Mississippi River. I closed my eyes and took in a deep breath, savoring the moment and daydreaming. Yep, this was my kind of town.

After another night in a motel, we crossed the river and drove on to Quincy, Illinois. Mom spent another day wall papering a few businesses as she called it, while Morris waited in the car with Rocky and me. I was starting to feel like I was riding with Bonnie Parker and Clyde Barrow, with the Federal Bureau of Investigation (FBI) in hot pursuit.

A pattern was developing with Morris' moods. He would wake up in the morning nervous and then pace the floor, looking out the curtains of the motel every few minutes. I think we all knew it was just a matter of time before the police closed in. By mid-afternoon, there was enough beer in his system that he became carefree and fun to be around. As the afternoon progressed, he would change to hard liquor. He became down-right mean, ready to fight man or beast. Mom knew his pattern well and tried to talk him into sticking with beer, but it just didn't happen.

Mom didn't drink alcohol other than an occasional beer with dinner. She started her mornings with a bottle of Coca-Cola and continued to drink them until bedtime. Morris complained that her habit was much more addictive and more expensive than his, but I wished they would both just stick with Coca-Cola.

✻

It was a beautiful Saturday night when we entered Springfield, Illinois. The sun had just gone below the horizon, leaving the clouds above the city a beautiful pink.

The main street through town was busy with teenagers in nice cars, while other groups walked the sidewalks, waving at the honking cars that passed by. A group of girls saw me looking out the back window and waved with big smiles. I guess they thought I was older than I was. I sat up in the seat to look taller, smiled and waved back. If I had to live in a large city, this would be a good choice.

A teenager in a 1955 Ford Fairlane convertible, all decked out with chrome, stopped beside us at a red light. The driver looked to be about 18 or 19 years old, his black hair slicked back in an Elvis look. He glanced over at our 1950 Ford V8 Coupe, grinned and revved his motor twice, like he wanted to race. Morris answered his challenge by doing the same.

When the light turned green, Morris popped the clutch and the race was on. The tires were screaming and the air filled with the smell of burnt rubber. We were going through town at 70 miles per hour, with both cars side by side. Mom was screaming at the top of her lungs.
"Damn it Morris, what the hell are you trying to prove? You've got kids in the car. Now just knock it off before you kill us."

Morris seemed to be in a trance, with just one thing on his mind; winning the race at any risk. Rocky and I were laughing, and that seemed to encourage him to go even faster. Mom glared at us, as if to say, "shut up!"

Each red light we came to became the same ritual, with grins exchanged and motors racing at full throttle. Morris would stomp the accelerator to the floor, slamming gears. We would literally fly over dips in the street at the intersections. Demented fire burned in Mom's eyes, but Morris was totally ignoring her yelling and screaming, focused only on out running the other car.

At the next traffic light, Morris and his competitor stopped, ready to do it all again. Mom jumped out dragging Rocky with her and yelled for me to get out too.

When the light turned green again, we were left standing in a cloud of smoke and burnt rubber as the two cars raced off down the street and disappeared into the darkness. We waited there in silence with Mom wiping away tears. We could still hear the faint roar of cars racing in the distance.

"I hope the stupid son-of-a-bitch kills himself." Mom called Morris every name she could think of while we waited for him to finish playing and come back for us. I'm surprised Mom waited at all, but where could we go? When he did come back, he had a sour look on his face, so I knew he must have lost the race.

We rode along for miles in complete silence; Mom staring out the window into the darkness. Only the songs playing on the radio broke the stillness that had enveloped our car. At the next town we came to, Mom complained that we hadn't eaten and the kids must be starved. She looked back at me and asked if I was hungry, knowing I would say yes.

"Have you ever heard that kid say no to food?" Morris grumbled.

I didn't answer, knowing anything I said would result in another rude remark.

Mom spotted an Italian restaurant and wanted to stop there, but Morris just kept going. For the next few miles, Mom let him have it with both barrels. "You know you're really a selfish person. You only think about yourself; you have no regard for anyone else. If a cop had seen you driving like you did back there and checked us out, where do you think I would be? See Morris—you just don't think about anyone but yourself."

Morris didn't try to defend himself, but turned his bottle of Vodka up and took a long four gurgle drink.

"Morris, I asked you to stop at that Italian restaurant. I can't believe you're just going to let the kids go hungry."

With no warning, he slammed the brakes on and the car slid sideways down the highway with Mom screaming. Before the car had stopped completely, Morris popped the clutch, and drove through the median into the southbound lanes, quickly picking up speed—70—80 then 90 miles per hour. Mom begged him to slow down, but he didn't seem to be listening.

"Morris, please just stop and let us out. You're going to kill us if you keep driving like this." Mom's screams and pleas fell on deaf ears. He drove back to the Italian restaurant and slid to a stop in the parking lot in a cloud of dust.

"Are you happy now?—goddamn it!" He screamed, punching the dashboard with his fist.

I wondered if anyone ever told him that one of God's 10 Commandments said: *"Thou shalt not take the name of the Lord thy God in vain."* I wasn't going to be the one to tell him. Not now anyway.

Mom and Morris were still arguing as we went inside the restaurant. The waitress and other customers were watching us as we sat down at a table, ignoring the wait to be seated sign.

It was a beautiful restaurant, with a rich decor. We all had spaghetti except for Morris. He just sat there fuming, drinking beer after beer.

"Morris, you need to eat something," Mom suggested. "You know how you get if you drink a lot on an empty stomach, and you haven't had anything since this morning."

I knew Mom should just back off and leave him alone. In the short time I'd been around him, I knew when to keep my mouth shut. I couldn't understand why she just never seemed to figure that out.

Mom was kind of a food critic. If the meal was good, she would tip the waitress and the cook. Sometimes she would even ask the waitress to have the cook come to our table. If the food was bad, you could count on Mom letting someone know. Unfortunately, this had to be one of those times when she complained.

"They call this an Italian restaurant, and they don't even know how to fix something as simple as spaghetti. Look at this shit," she grumbled. "How does yours taste, Cliff?" she asked.

"It tastes good to me. If you're not going to finish yours, can I have it?" Morris gave me a despicable look. I knew I shouldn't have said anything.

"You want two more servings, you goddamn glutton?" he said, loud enough that the people around us could hear.

His words caused a knot in my stomach. I just hung my head, too embarrassed to answer. I expected Mom to defend me, but she just gave him a hard look and shook her head with a disgusted look on her face. Looking around, she glared at the other customers that were watching us.

The sick feeling in my stomach grew, and I lost my appetite. I was just moving my spaghetti around with my fork, watching Morris out of the corner of my eye, wondering what he was going to say next.

"I don't think they even know what chocolate malt is," Mom complained. "Just look at this crap. It's not even thick. That lazy bitch of a waitress hasn't even been back to see how we're doing. I'm going to talk to the damn manager."

It was embarrassing enough with Morris acting like he was without Mom starting too.

With no warning, Morris grabbed the milkshake away from Mom and dumped the whole thing on her head. She had thick globs of ice cream in her hair with more running down her face. Everyone in the restaurant was watching with their mouths open in disbelief. Morris grabbed Mom by the arm and started dragging her toward the door as she fought to pull free, screaming and crying with Rocky and me following behind in tears.

The manager met us at the door demanding payment for the meal. We stopped at the counter long enough for the waitress to bring our bill, and Mom to scratch out another check.

"We don't take out of state checks," the manager announced, as he studied the worthless paper in his hand.

"Well, by God, you're taking this one!" Mom snapped, as we continued out the door.

I was wishing I was back in Bridge City and wondered how far it was back to the Mississippi River. How long would it take to drift to the Gulf of Mexico?

CHAPTER

TWENTY-FIVE

We were back to silence in the car as Morris continued driving north. I could hear mom crying softly. That too stopped when Morris yelled, "Stop your damned whimpering and turn the volume up on the radio!"

Morris drove for another four or five hours stopping once for gas and another for a bottle of vodka. We passed right through Chicago without stopping. Eager to get out of the car, I was afraid to say anything and was relieved when Mom asked why we didn't get a motel and stop for the night.

Morris seemed to be trying to make up for the way he had acted and asked if we would like to find a motel on the shore of Lake Michigan. We all liked that idea, and even more so when he said we could probably stay there for a few days. We all needed a break. It was time to get out of the car for awhile.

We finally stopped at a nice motel just south of Kenosha, Wisconsin, right on a high bank overlooking Lake Michigan. To my disappointment, it was too dark to see the water.

Mom and Morris were still sleeping when I awoke the next morning. I slipped out of the room and was feeding potato chips to sea gulls before the morning sun rose from the water, like a large orange egg yoke. All at once the clouds caused the yoke to burst and spill over the horizon in beautiful colors. There was water as far as I could see. I had to remind myself, this is not an ocean—it's a lake. But boy what a lake it was. Beautiful blue water as far as the eye can see.

After Mom and Morris woke up, we all went out for a big breakfast and then played on the beach waiting for the sun to warm the water.

Around noon, it was back to work. Morris drove Mom around town as she wrote checks to every business that she could con into accepting them. It amazed me that she could write checks all over the country with out of state identification. Not only was she not nervous about doing it, but she seemed to take great pride in her ability to pull it off. Morris was just the opposite and seemed to drink to build his courage. The more checks she wrote, the more he drank.

Late that afternoon the alcohol had its normal effect and Morris became crude with his comments again. Mom decided to call it a day, as she didn't want another public display of his demeanor and suggested we go back to the motel.

Rocky and I immediately went down to the beach and started playing in the water. Morris must have grown tired of fighting with Mom, because he came down to the beach and started playing with us. He wanted to take Rocky into the deeper water, but Rocky was afraid and starting crying and tried to pull away. Morris became furious. He grabbed Rocky by the arm and pulled him back to the motel room, with Rocky screaming the whole way.

Mom tried to come to Rocky's aid, but Morris hit her in the face, knocking her back onto the bed. I wanted so badly to jump in and stop him, but I was afraid to do anything. Why did she stay with him, I asked myself? After all, she was the one risking her freedom to earn an income, and he was just drinking it up as fast as she made it.

It was hard to just stand there while he hit my Mom and not do anything. But what could I do? If I tried to stop him, he would probably beat me too. I could run to the office and call the police, but that was probably the last thing Mom would want. If the police checked her out, they would arrest her and what would they do with us?

I couldn't stand to watch his abuse. Leaving Mom and Rocky in the room crying, I walked back down to the lake and gazed out at the water through my tears. I hated Morris for the way he treated us.

The afternoon quickly passed as I occupied my time dragging poles together to construct a small raft. I scavenged enough material from the beach and the back of the motel to hold everything together.

A few hours later Morris came back to the beach, and I talked him into going for a cruise on my boat. He was drunk enough not to be afraid and climbed onboard the newly christened *Cajun Queen II*.

I only planned to take him out a short distance, but the wind came up and was blowing us out to sea. Well, maybe not sea as this is a lake, but from the size of the waves breaking over the raft, you would have thought it was the ocean. Morris was in a panic and holding on for dear life, while I was having a blast and loving every minute of it. I was in my element.

"Let me show you something Papaw taught me," I told Morris

with all the confidence of a true Cajun sea captain. If the raft breaks apart, you can take off your jeans and make an emergency life preserver with them." Standing up on the raft, I pulled off my jeans and tied knots in both legs, demonstrating how it was done. "Then you zip the jeans back up, place a pant leg under each arm, and jump in like this!" I landed in the water cannon ball style and floated up and down the waves on my self-made life preserver. "Try it—its fun," I yelled.

"Son, I don't know if you're doing this on purpose or not, but I'm afraid. I don't know how to swim. I know I've said and done some mean things to you and your Mom, and I'm sorry. Please, get us back to shore," Morris begged.

I ducked my head into the water, so he wouldn't see the smile that covered my face.

I had to keep tightening the ropes holding the *Cajun Queen II* together to keep her from breaking up. You could see the panic in his eyes each time I stood up and dove off the raft. "Please Cliff, I wish you wouldn't do that. You're going to make the raft fall apart."

His begging me to stop, only added to my fun. "I'm just diving to see how far the bottom is, so I could tell if we are getting closer to the shore or not." I'd surface behind Morris and make him wonder what had happened to me.

"I can't dive deep enough to even see the bottom!" I said, unable to hold back a grin. "But at least we don't have to worry about sharks." It was kind of nice to be the captain and have control over someone I had always been frightened of. I liked having that power for a change.

"Holy Cow, Look how close those ships are!" I yelled to Morris. I thought he was going to start crying. They looked closer than the shore.

"Do you know what state we will be in if we float all the way across the lake?" I asked. He didn't acknowledge my question, but I answered anyway—"Michigan!"

It took some convincing to talk Morris into getting in the water and help kick, but I told him that was the only way we would make it to shore.

We could barely see Mom's silhouette standing on the bluff waving her arms as the sun fell low on the horizon. A few hours later, cold and tired we stumbled on the beach, like survivors from some lost at sea movie. Totaled exhausted, we climbed up the bluff as the red sun went down in the western sky.

With a smile on my face, I fought back a chuckle. You know the old saying: "A red sky at night is a sailor's delight." This had been a delightful afternoon, and I felt a new inner-strength, I had never experienced before. I hoped Mom and Rocky enjoyed their peaceful afternoon together.

CHAPTER

TWENTY-SIX

A s we traveled the country I can't begin to count the number of times we would stop in towns along the way so Mom could write more checks. This trip had taken us as far north as Madison, Wisconsin, then we turned south and followed the Mississippi River to the Gulf Coast. At last we turned west toward Texas. It seemed like we had been traveling for a year. I had lost track of even what month it was, but then it really didn't matter.

A lot of the conversations between Mom and Morris concerned settling down somewhere so Rocky and I could start school. They both worried that stopping would mean getting caught, and transferring school records would point to where we were. Mom reasoned if we returned to a school where we had been before, registration may not become a large obstacle.

The possibilities flew through my head as fast as the towns we drove through. In Texas I had been to school in Bridge City, Deweyville and Pasadena. Then there was Burlington, Colorado, Cove in Arkansas and Seminole, Oklahoma. That would make six possible places to pick from. Their discussions always occurred when Rocky and I were supposed to be sleeping. I wanted to add my choices of favorite places to live, but I didn't think they would be influenced by my suggestions anyway.

We had just passed through Lafayette, Louisiana when I noticed the sign announcing Lake Charles 75 miles—Beaumont 130. I hadn't really cared where we were until I saw the sign, but now I was at attention. They must have decided on Bridge City and that suited me just fine. I watched as the bridges and towns went by, Crowley, Jennings and Lake Charles and then my Sabine River. We were back in territory I was familiar with. It was going to be great to see Grandma and my old friends again.

We entered Orange, Texas and soon a sign announced the turn off for Bridge City and Port Arthur, but to my dismay, Morris just kept driving.

"Hey, you missed your turn," I pointed out. My excitement was met by silence. I could see a problem in Mom's face, and she could see the disappointment in mine.

"Cliff, the police may be watching Grandma's. I hope you understand why we can't go there. We just can't take a chance like that."

Yea, I understood alright. I understood I didn't want to go another dang mile. I wanted to ask if they could just drop me off, but I was afraid to. Here we were right back where I want to be, and we don't even stop. I could walk to Grandma's and live with her, and I'm sure she would be glad to see me. Maybe I should act like I needed to go to the bathroom. We would stop at a gas station, and I could just run away. Mom would know where I went, and would be afraid to come after me.

Many thoughts passed through my head, as the distance between us and Bridge City grew. They weren't good thoughts either. Most of them involved running away. Instead, I didn't do anything but watch familiar country pass by and soak it in. I was tired of living in the car. The need to be free pulled at my heart, and I ached from confinement. It was starting to feel like the highway would never end.

We drove right through Houston without even calling Verna or Uncle Mel. I thought if Mom was worried about the cops watching their apartment, we could at least call them, and see if they wanted to meet us somewhere.

By the time we got to El Paso, I really was convinced the highway was endless. I must have died and was really in hell. This was my punishment for stealing a Christmas tree and a headstone. I couldn't ask the old familiar question of, "When will we be there?" because no one in the car knew where we were going.

When we got to Las Cruces, New Mexico, Mom shared her plan with us. We would go to Las Vegas, Nevada and her and Morris would turn the cash she made over the past three months, into enough money to buy us a nice home. For the next 800 miles Mom talked about how nice our home would be. She would buy us both bicycles and new clothes; we would each have our own room. No more traveling and sleeping in different beds each night. Home cooked meals again, and on weekends she promised we could go to the movies. Life would be better than it ever had been.

"So, where are we going to live I asked?" Guessing she would answer California.

"Well, Morris grew up in Burlington, and he knows everyone there. He shouldn't have any problem finding a job. Your Grandma and Grandpa Mac will sure be glad to see you kids. Plus, you and Rocky both have school records there, so it shouldn't be a problem to get you both registered."

"But I have school records in Bridge City too," I protested. "And won't the police be watching in Burlington too?" My question was ignored. My heart sank. How could they do this to me? Burlington was the last place in the world I wanted to go.

✿

The bright lights of Las Vegas took my breath away. Maybe Mom would like Las Vegas and we could just live here, I reasoned. We drove down the strip, and watched the bright lights while looking for a place to stay. Morris spotted a motel named the Kit Carson and thought it was a good luck sign. After all, Burlington, Colorado is in Kit Carson County. Mom said we needed all the luck we could get. The sign offering free ice was a plus, so we rented a room there.

Each day became the same monotonous routine. Mom and Morris gambled while Rocky and I stayed in the motel room and watched television. They picked us up for dinner and then we'd go back to the motel to be dropped off again while they gambled. Sometime during the night they would come in, but we normally didn't hear them unless they were fighting.

We had been in Las Vegas for five days, and Mom was slowly losing her money. With her not winning, I didn't hold much hope of us living here. I was to the point where I didn't care too much for Vegas anyway. The more money Mom and Morris lost, the crankier they both became.

We were sitting at a red light in downtown Las Vegas one evening when a car plowed into the rear end of our car. I looked back and saw a red headed lady stick her head out the driver's window yelling, but we couldn't hear what she was saying. A lady sitting on the passenger side seemed to be trying to quiet her down, but they were both laughing. When Morris opened his door to get out, I heard the lady yell again.

"Get the hell out of the way, I'm from Montana. Move that piece of shit before I ram it again."

Mom was fighting mad, and jumped out of the car. Morris let out an, "Oh shit!" and jumped out, grabbing Mom at the back of our car. He struggled to hold her back, and reminded her that she was too hot for the police to be called. She needed to shut the hell up and stay in the car unless she wanted to go back to jail.

About then the lady yelled: "Come on bitch, you think you're bad. I'll show you what a Montana redhead can do, and then I'll steal your old man."

That's all it took. Mom pushed passed Morris and had the redhead knocked to the pavement and was on top of her before Morris could respond. Mom would have probably beaten the redhead to death if Morris hadn't pulled her off.

The sound of sirens approaching brought Mom back to her senses. Mom and Morris jumped back in our car and we raced off. I looked back and saw the lady was still lying in the street beside her car, and she wasn't moving. Her passenger had a shocked look and seemed unsure of what to do. She was just coming out the passenger side as we sped away.

"I hope to hell she didn't get our license plate number," Morris groaned while watching his rearview mirror.

Other than some busted tail lights and a dented trunk, there wasn't too much damage to our car. Mom was still cussing and suggested leaving Las Vegas for somewhere with less stupid people.

"And where the hell would that be?" Morris asked, unsure where to point the car. There was silence in the car as he waited for an answer.

I wanted to say; "I know—Bridge City." but I knew it wouldn't do any good.

"Reno, Nevada, the biggest little city in the world," Mom replied with a smile. You remember how well we did in Harold's Club the last time don't you?"

"Yea, I remember," Morris answered, "But I liked the Nevada Club better."

We stopped by the motel just long enough to pack and were on the road again. I fell asleep listening to Mom gripe about the dame in the short skirt that Morris had been making goo-goo eyes at in the casino in Vegas.

"That's bull shit," Morris replied.

"Morris I can see right through you. You're not fooling anyone. I saw you watching her every move. You had lust pouring out your ears and your tongue hung out like a dog."

"You're full of shit. It's just a natural reaction to look when you see someone dressed like that," he argued.

We drove most of the night and were soon back to the same routine in Reno. They both gambled, while Rocky and I stayed in the motel watching television.

After just a few days there, Mom's money was almost gone. In one last bid for wealth, Mom decided to gamble with the casino's money. She would write each casino the largest check they would be willing to take. For the plan to work, she would wait until Friday after the banks were closed, then we would be out of the state when they opened Monday morning.

"Oh sure," Morris moaned; "You've got the police looking for us all over the country. You may as well add the damn Mafia, too."

"You know Morris, you always bitch and moan about how I make the money, but you damn sure don't have a problem with spending what I make!" Mom yelled.

Mom's plan of cashing checks at all the casinos worked. By late Sunday night we were in Utah, headed for Colorado. Mom was pleased with herself for pulling off her scam. Morris was drunk, and Rocky was sleeping. I was dreading our destination, but most of all I hated having to go back to school in Burlington. Why couldn't it be anywhere else? Maybe we would get lucky and break down in some small Colorado town in the mountains.

CHAPTER
TWENTY-SEVEN

The house we bought in Burlington was a large two story at the edge of town. It looked fine to me but Mom said it was going to need a lot of work. According to her, it needed painted both inside and out, the appliances and cabinets needed to be updated, and the lawn was hideous.

Morris found a job working for a local farmer. It didn't pay a lot, but at least it provided an income. Unfortunately Morris' pay checks just weren't big enough to cover Mom's plans for the house. Soon she was taking out-of-town trips and passing checks to cover the improvements to our house.

It wasn't long before the house had new paint, and all our furniture and appliances were brand new. Just like Mom had promised, Rocky and I both had new bicycles and a full wardrobe of nice clothes.

Morris tried to slow Mom down on her out-of-town check writing trips, but she was convinced there was no way the checks could ever be traced back to her. She was using fake identification and traveled far enough from Burlington that no one would ever recognize her. Morris couldn't say a lot because Mom was definitely bringing in a lot more money than he was. And he sure didn't mind his new recliner, the stereo or the new television.

Mom's check writing became almost as addictive as Morris' need for alcohol. It's been said that all con-artists look for that score of a life time. For some it's the dollar signs flashing in their eyes but for others, it's the thrill of knowing they pulled off their biggest scam yet. I would have thought the casinos in Reno would have been Mom's big score, but hers came at a hardware store in Colby, Kansas.

Like all the other stores she had visited, she walked up to the counter with a few items for our house and her checkbook ready. No one was around the cash register. Apparently, all the employees must have been in the back room. She stood there for awhile, patiently waiting, and that's when she spotted it on the counter within easy reach—a business checkbook. Mom glanced around twice just to make sure it was safe, then immediately slipped the checkbook under her sweater and walked out the front door.

After having business cards printed, Mom passed herself off as being the new owner of the business. Using the name on her fake identification card, she was ready to do some serious check writing. Her check writing trips had to be performed when the banks were closed, so no one could verify funds. Western Kansas, Nebraska and Eastern Colorado were hit hard for weeks. Mom really had a gift of gab and played her part well. No one expected a nice looking business owner with such a pleasant personality would be deceitful.

Mom's out of town trips became frequent. On weekends we would be rewarded with trips to the stock car races in Kansas and Nebraska, or sometimes even the Lakeside Amusement Park in Denver.

Sometimes we would get home so late on Sunday nights; we would have a hard time getting up for school on Monday mornings. The first time I came home with bad grades, Mom beat my butt. I guess she never considered that changing schools so often, had any effect on my grades.

When it was time to bring my report card home again, I only had a few F's. Out of necessity, I devised a way to prevent that from ever happening again. No, I didn't study harder. I just copied Mom's techniques and forged my report card. If I were caught, I could say; "I was just copying you, Mom." It may work, or then again she may just beat me to death.

Taking an ink pen, I turned F's into B's. Mom and Morris were proud of how well I was doing, but wanted me to bring those D- and D's up next time. Some of the D's did come up to C's on the next report card from my trying harder but the D- went to an F. Of course I changed it to a B before I went home. An outstanding improvement!

The hard part was erasing my extra lines before I took the report card back to school. The next quarter I had to draw them back in place, and erase them again before returning to school. Having a good report card was sure turning into a big hassle.

I was really surprised the next time we took report cards home. My F's magically had the B already drawn in place. The question haunted my mind all weekend. Should I erase it before I go back to school? The teacher must know what I'm doing and it's a trap, I reasoned. Maybe I didn't erase the ink well enough last time and the ink bled back through. Possibly, the teacher knew how bad I had it at home and was just helping me out.

However it happened, the paper on the report card was getting too thin from all the erasing, so I just left the B in place and nothing was ever said.

✦✦✦

I didn't like the fake rich kid lifestyle I was being forced into. I liked running barefoot exploring the countryside, and swimming in canals. It just wasn't natural to be restricted to a house and small yard with more rules than I could remember. I couldn't even pee outside without getting in trouble. I hated having to wear cowboy boots that were too narrow for my wide feet but Mom just kept buying them anyway. Mom expected me to keep myself, my brother and the house clean at all times. I felt like the only reason they wanted me, was to have someone to do the chores and watch Rocky.

One day Mom didn't like the dishwashing job I had done. I was just getting out of the shower when she appeared with one of Morris' leather cowboy belts. Before I could get my clothes on, she began delivering swift, hard blows to my wet backside. It was the worse beating I had ever experienced. My whole body screamed in sheer agony, and the pain was nauseating. Blood rushed to my brain, making my ears pop as I fought to pull free. The torture continued until she passed out from exhaustion. I stood over her, unsure of what to do.

When she regained consciousness, the beating started all over again until she physically wore herself out.

My backside was raw and covered with raised welts that

turned to bruises the next day. These beatings continued on a regular basis. If Morris were there, he would try to stop her but he risked getting hurt himself. She would work herself into an out of control rage. Morris would have to actually grab her arms and hold them to get the belt away from her. She would call me every name she could think of. It seemed like almost anything would set her off. I couldn't understand why she hated me.

Just a few weeks later, after another severe beating, Mom drug me out of the house screaming; "Get out!"

I thought she was kicking me out of the house and expected me to leave. I went out the front gate, and started walking east on Highway 24 towards Kansas. Hot tears flowed down my cheeks. I didn't know where to go or what to do. I was in a daze, wishing someone—no anyone, loved me. If there had been a river near, I'm sure I would have found some comfort there. The plains of Colorado didn't offer many choices; nothing but barbed wire fences and tumbleweeds.

Texas was heavy on my mind when Mom pulled up in the car. I wanted to run, but thought maybe she came to apologize. Instead, she started beating me all over again for trying to run away.

"But you told me to leave," I begged as she hit me repeatedly. My body ached from the pain.

"Get your ass in the car, now!" she screamed.

That night I knelt down beside my bed and prayed: *"God, maybe it's wrong for me to ask this, but would you please put my Mom back in prison?"*

I know that's a terrible thing to pray, but I felt that was my only hope. I needed help in a big way, and God was always there for me in the past. All I had to do was ask and believe. Even today as I think back, it grips me in a strange way – as if saying that prayer had the power to force the future in a chosen direction.

In just a few days my prayers were answered. The Kansas Bureau of Investigation had tracked Mom down and placed her under arrest. A fake ID card may change your name, but it doesn't change your fingerprints.

Mom's arrest was featured on the nightly news and the front page of the local newspaper. It was my fault. My prayer made it happen.

The next day at school, a boy in my class walked up to me with a sneer on his face. He was one of the more popular kids; his dad a successful business person. I could tell whatever he was going to say wouldn't be nice. The look on his face begged to be punched before he opened his mouth, but I fought back the urge.

"Hey Cliff, we saw your mom on television last night."

"Yeah—what about it?" I answered, ready to defend the reputation I didn't have.

"My dad said she's going to prison for a long, l-o-n-g time," he answered with the same smirk on his face.

He said it in more of a "ha ha ha" tone of voice. Little did he or anyone else know that I was glad she was gone.

Regardless of how I felt, he needed to be hit, and my fist connected with his chin. He fell back and landed on the ground crying. I turned and walked off, knowing he wouldn't fight back, but also to escape the looks from the other kids who had begun crowding around. I'm sure he told them why I punched him. With his big mouth, everyone in the school would soon know about my Mom.

The bell rang, signaling recess was over. I had just sat down at my desk, before the other kids even got in the room, when the principal walked in.

"Cliff, come with me. We're not going to tolerate this kind of behavior in this school. What seems to be your problem?" he asked.

I knew telling him wouldn't help, because he took his paddle off the wall before I even had a chance to answer. He stood towering over me while my eyes studied the 1/8 inch holes drilled in his paddle to inflict additional pain.

"Do you have anything you'd like to say before I use this?" He asked.

Kiss my ass, crossed my mind, but instead I just answered, "No sir."

The principal brought his paddle down hard against my butt with enough force to push me forward, but he couldn't make me cry. The truth was, no pain he could inflict would be as hurtful as what I had already experienced.

The whipping, the stares from my classmates, none of it mattered. The rumors soon spread throughout the school, and everywhere I went, kids were whispering to each other and looking at me.

On weekends, Morris drove us to Colby, Kansas to visit Mom. Seeing her there, locked in a small cell all by herself only made me feel worse. Each night I prayed for forgiveness, as I felt it was my prayers that put her there. I told God he didn't have to keep her locked up. I was just tired of her beatings, and I didn't want to live with her or stay in Burlington.

The jail was a small concrete building, overgrown with vines and located beside the courthouse. The building looked like it had been there for a hundred years. A huge iron door facing the Court House was the entrance to the women's side, while the door to the men's side was just around the corner.

Inside the jail, a hallway with another door separated the men from the women's side. The hallway door had a slit about five or six inches tall and two feet wide so the jailer could slip trays of food into the cell without opening the door.

Mom was the only female prisoner and was forbidden to have any contact with the men. However, if she moved to the far side of her cell, and the men happened to be in the hallway, it was possible for her to see them.

The prisoners on the men's side all came into the hallway during one of our weekend visits, and Mom introduced us to them. One guy named Frank, seemed friendlier than the others.

Morris kept his voice down so the other men couldn't hear him, but he was upset that Mom had spent hours talking to Frank and was upset that they knew each other so well. Morris said he was going to talk to the sheriff about putting up a solid door between them. Mom's face turned red and she exploded in a guiltless rage, loud enough for everyone to hear.

"Morris, you listen to me! Frank's in here for burglary. Just like me, he's sentenced to the penitentiary, and he's planning to get us out of here. I haven't seen you lift a damn finger to do anything to help. Now just shut the hell up about the damn door or you're going to screw up our plans. I'm looking at a lot of years that I don't intend to do. It will be easier to escape from here than wait until I'm in prison."

Morris instantly backed down and when he asked how they planned to get out, Mom told Rocky and I to go outside and play for a few minutes so they could talk in private.

Why was it anytime the conversations got interesting we were sent outside to play? There wasn't anything to do outside on the courthouse lawn, and Rocky was irritated because I wouldn't play with him. My mind was on just one thing; Mom's plan to escape. Were we going to move somewhere with her or would she leave us behind?

All week long I couldn't concentrate on my school work. I wondered if the police would show up at our house looking for Mom, or worse yet, the school. How would we know she had made good on her escape plan? I guess we would see it on television or hear it on the radio.

The next Sunday we went to visit Mom again, not knowing for sure if she was still there. Mom was upset because her escape plan had failed.

We learned that Frank had stripped naked, gotten soaking wet and soaped himself down. Then he had attempted to slide through the food tray slot in the hall door. He had planned to hide and wait for the sheriff's wife to bring in breakfast. He promised Mom he wouldn't hurt the lady, but he'd just take her keys, free Mom and lock the sheriff's wife in Mom's cell. Frank's girlfriend would be waiting in a car near the jail and they would take Mom anywhere she wanted to go.

Such a simple plan, but something happened they hadn't planned on. Frank got stuck halfway through the narrow opening in the door and was still hanging there in pain, bare butt naked, when the sheriff's wife arrived in the morning. Frank was moved to a more secure jail in a neighboring county.

I suggested that Morris could borrow a John Deere tractor from his boss, then back up to the jail and pull Mom's window out with a log chain. Again, I was sent outside to play.

God answered part of my prayers two weeks later when Morris decided it would be best to take me back to Big Mama's. I was pleased with Morris' wise decision and knew there must have been some divine intervention going on. Maybe he was afraid I would make plans to run away again. Whatever the reason, I couldn't wait to get out of there.

Chapter TWENTY-EIGHT

R ain was coming down in sheets as we crossed the Sabine River into Louisiana, and it continued raining all the way to Big Mama's. The house sat up on a small hill overlooking Highway 8. The map I had been studying showed a town there named Caney, but it was really just the intersection of another secondary highway and four houses. According to the map, Anacoco Lake was just a short distance through the thick stand of pine trees.

As we pulled into the driveway, Big Mama came out on the front porch with a rifle in her hand to greet us.

"I hope that crazy old bitty doesn't shoot us," Morris said with a look of concern on his face. She looked older and more wrinkled than I remembered. On the other hand, Papaw still looked the same. I had to smile as he took the gun away from her. Boy, they sure hadn't changed.

After the hugs and handshakes, a celebration was in order. Morris and Papaw drove the nine miles into Leesville to replenish the liquor supply. Morris and Big Mama had their differences in the past, but alcohol was one thing they had in common. I couldn't imagine them getting drunk together since they were such opposites. When Morris was drunk he would be loud and boisterous, while Papaw was quiet and reserved. And Big Mama—well no one wanted to be around her when she was drunk. She became mean and unpredictable, like a snake, ready to lash out at anything close, often for no reason.

They drank into the night and I listened in on a few of their conversations, as I lay in my new bedroom trying to sleep. Big Mama blamed Morris for Mom being in prison. Morris blamed her upbringing, the hunger in her eyes and always wanting more that he could provide. Papaw just tried to keep peace between them and had his hands full.

When they finally decided to call it a night, Morris told Papaw he would be leaving in the morning. Big Mama flew into a name calling rage.

"So you're just going to dump Cliff off like some stray dog? Let me tell you something Morris, you're nothing but a worthless son-of-a-bitch. That's all you've ever been and that's all you'll ever be. Cliff's always welcome to stay with us, but I don't like the way you've gone about it. You're a spineless wonder Morris. You should really be proud of yourself."

I heard a bang against the wall and then what sounded like a beer can bouncing across the wooden floor. I guessed she must have thrown a beer can and missed her target.

Morris had enough and knew it was hopeless to argue with her. He came into my bedroom and closed the door. He fixed himself a pallet next to the open window, taking full advantage of the light breeze that stirred the curtains. The faint fragrance of a Magnolia tree drifted through the evening air. We were soon both fast asleep, exhausted from our long trip.

About an hour later I awoke to a hissing sound. A snake was my first thought. The sound was coming from the direction where Morris was sleeping. His pallet was close enough that I could reach his feet without getting off the bed, but I didn't want to chance getting bit. I pulled on his toes until he sprang up to a sitting position. His look of surprise was visible in the moonlight.

"What the hell is going on?" he asked bewildered.

"I can hear a snake," I whispered.

Morris shot up from the floor and landed on the bed with me, as we both scanned the hardwood floor where he had been laying.

"Can you see anything?" I asked.

"No, it's too dark, but I can hear it too. It sounds like it's outside," Morris answered, still unsure.

Morris bravely stood up and tiptoed to the window. Without saying a word, he turned and ran outside. Surely he's not going to try and catch a snake in the dark.

I sprang to the window to watch.

To my surprise, the hissing was Big Mama letting the air out of the tires on Morris' car. She was still in a squatting position, when Morris came up behind her. He kicked her hard in the butt with his barefoot. She let out a scream and rolled forward, stunned. Morris was still cussing as she staggered toward the house.

"You're a dead son-of-a-bitch Morris. If my husband doesn't kill you then by God, I'll do it myself."

Morris surveyed the damage to his tires, and determined they still had enough air to be driven a short distance. We said our good-byes through the open window.

As Morris headed down the driveway, Big Mama reappeared with the rifle. It was too late. He was already at the bottom of the driveway and had turned toward Texas. Big Mama brought the rifle up to her shoulder and pulled the trigger anyway, sending a bullet into the trees across the highway. Thank God no one was driving by at the time.

⟡

Again, I was allowed to skip the remaining month of school with the promise I could easily make it up next year. After all, I told Big Mama; I was almost a straight A student in Burlington. Besides, I had enough bad school experiences to last me a lifetime, so why rush back into it if I didn't have to?

The next day I started exploring my new surroundings. Anacoco Lake was closer than I had thought, and Sandy Creek was just a quarter of a mile down the highway with Caney Creek the other direction.

It felt so good to have my freedom back, and at every opportunity I explored my new surroundings. The pirogue I found tied under the Sandy Creek Bridge was more than luck. It was almost as if some greater power had left it there for my use. At first it was just a few short trial runs to see how well the boat handled. Soon I had all of Sandy Creek explored and started doing full day trips on Anacoco Lake.

A pirogue or "Cajun Canoe," as many people call them, are popular in the marshes and bayous of Louisiana. I named this one the *"Cajun Queen III,"* keeping with the tradition of the previous boats in my life. I was hesitant to paint the name on the boat, for fear the real owner wouldn't approve.

❦

It was bound to happen. One day the pirogue was missing from under the bridge. That boat had practically become mine, and I was in disbelief to discover it gone. Well maybe I would find out who I had been sharing the pirogue with after all, and just maybe, I could get permission to use it. Carefully I worked my way through the thick brush trying to catch a glimpse of the person. Just around the first bend on Sandy Creek, I found the *Cajun Queen III* tied to an old dead tree that was partially submerged in the water. Not moving, I froze in the thick brush, surveying my surroundings to make sure no one was around.

The entanglement of the thicket along the bank made the boat hard to get to, so when I finished using it, I tied the boat back under the bridge where it belonged.

I guess it shouldn't have come as a surprise to find it chained under the bridge with a padlock the next time I went to use it. With disgust, I stared at the lock. Hadn't I always returned the boat to the bridge when I was finished with it? I was the one who kept it clean and the water bailed out. I was always careful to remove any mud or leaves that may have been tracked in.

I just couldn't believe someone would put a chain and lock on the boat, especially as well as it had been cared for. I had even taken the time to sand and varnish the paddle, and now it was gone. If he thought that was going to change anything, well he'd better just think again. I would just make my own paddle.

An eye bolt went through the bow of the boat with a nut on the inside and a thick chain went through the eye of the bolt, and was wrapped twice around one of the bridge pilings. After studying the situation, I found a solution that would work.

It meant walking back to the house and returning with pliers and a crescent wrench, but it was no great challenge to unscrew the bolt and use the boat anytime I wanted to. I just had to remember to bring a few tools with me when I wanted to use it. Whoever thought the pirogue was for their exclusive use was just going to learn how to share. After all, I had squatter's rights.

Paddling cautiously up Sandy Creek with a homemade paddle, I was at peace with my surroundings. Silently, I would sneak up on the turtles that lined up on fallen logs, soaking up the warm sunshine. They would dive into the water at the sight of my pirogue approaching with a splash. Dragonfly's hummed above the water and lulled me into a dream-like trance, and then took flight as the bow of the boat cut gently through the lily pads. The stillness would occasionally be broken by a frog diving for cover under the water's surface or a woodpecker hammering its beak into a dead tree above the creek.

Day after day, I paddled slowly up Sandy Creek, never tiring of the tranquil bliss. Sometimes I lay in the bottom of the boat, letting it gently drift while I napped in the warm sun. Crickets would sing to their heart's content. In the lonely quiet of the creek, I never once saw another person. Shallow enough to keep motorboats from going upstream, it was my secluded domain. A peaceful silence would descend, isolating me from the problems of my world.

Papaw knew how much I loved boats and was worried I was going to get caught using the pirogue. He paid $20.00 for an old rowboat, and moved it into a small cove on Anacoco Lake.

"You won't have to borrow the pirogue again," he reminded me.

Papaw was excited as he led me through the woods to where the boat was tied up. "Well, there she is. Have you decided what you're going to name her?"

"How does *Cajun Queen IV* sound?" I asked trying to seem excited. I was sure disappointed at what I saw. The old wooden boat was sunk to the bottom, with only the top edge of the gunnels above the water's surface. We waded out and lifted one side, allowing the tea colored water to rush over the opposite side. It leaked like a sieve, but Papaw must have known that, because he brought a coffee can with us to bail water. The boat was so big and bulky it was hard to move. Using a pole Papaw worked his way into Anacoco Lake as I continued to remove water. Anacoco Lake had so many trees and snags that it was really hard to maneuver without hitting one.

I forced myself to use the *Cajun Queen IV* a few times, but it was more work than fun. I was quick to abandon it and go back to using our pirogue. The remains of the boat are still resting in rot on the shore of Anacoco Lake.

Sometimes it would rain hard for days and Sandy Creek would overflow its banks, filling the mud-drenched flood plain along its shores with murky brown water. The water would come right up to the bottom the bridge and create small whirlpools as it passed the bridge pilings. Our boat would still be chained under the bridge but sunk to the bottom of the creek with no way to get to it. When the flood waters went down, it was always a job to pull the boat up on the bank and clean it—usually half full of black mud. I really hope the real owner appreciated the labor I donated to keep it ship shape. It was a fair trade off, I figured.

Over the summer, I found the boat hidden a few more times and decided that if he was going to hide it, then I could do the same.

෨෨෨

Saturday dawned clear with a beautiful sunrise. I was up early, as I planned to do some hunting along Sandy Creek. I wasn't far from the bridge, walking through the thick brush to where I had hidden the boat just a few days before. To my surprise, it wasn't where I had left it or any of the places it was normally hidden.

Maybe the person it really belonged to was using it. I was excited to at last have a chance to see what the person looked like, and possibly work a deal with him to continue using the boat. I moved very slowly through the brush being careful not to step on anything that would alert anyone on the creek.

Working my way through the underbrush, I spotted a rope tied to a tree root. The boat was almost completely covered with cut branches, making it almost impossible to see unless you knew where it was hidden.

I had just started to work my way to the boat when what sounded like a shotgun blast went off right behind me. The sound was still echoing through the woods as I dove for cover and took my gun off safety, ready to shoot back.

I was laying face down in the mud behind a tree with my heart beating so hard it should have registered as an earthquake on the Richter scale. The heavy scent of rich soil and damp moss filled my nostrils. I was almost afraid to raise my head and look around for fear I would get shot.

Crawling on my elbows, I made my way to a sweet gum tree for cover. Surely he wasn't going to shoot me for using his boat.

It took all the courage I had to look around, but no one was there. The eerie silence was broken only by the sound of my rapid breathing. The surrounding stillness was spooky. I felt my heart in my throat. Even the birds and crickets stopped singing. My mind flooded with all sorts of crazy thoughts, but the dead silence was broken when I heard people crying in the distance.

My mind raced with many possibilities. The crying was behind me near the bridge. Could someone have blown up the Sandy Creek Bridge? It was only about three hundred yards away.

Running through the brush as fast as I could, I came out of the woods right where a badly wrecked car sat smoking in the ditch. Small children in the car were crying, and I could hear screams coming from the ditch on the opposite side of the highway.

It looked like a scene from a disaster movie. A man was laying on the double yellow line of the highway, not moving and bleeding severely from a head wound. His buzzed head told me he was probably a soldier at near by Fort Polk. It was obvious he must have been ejected from one of the cars and landed there. I noticed a gold ring on his finger, and guessed his wife was in one of the cars. I was sure glad she couldn't see him this way. I just stood there in shock, not giving first aid—not knowing what to do.

A child screaming from the other car snapped me to my senses. I ran to their aid and found a woman and children bloody and crying. I was still unsure how to help.

The man in the center of the road seemed the most serious, so I ran back up on the highway and stood over him. A stream of blood was flowing from the center of the highway all the way to the graveled edge of the roadway, where it pooled in a small puddle and soaked in.

As the first car approached, I waved my arms in the air, signaling the people to stop. If they couldn't give first aid, at least they could go for help. We needed ambulances and fast!

Instead of stopping, the car sped up and raced around me, the driver hunched down where I could only see the top of his head. Puzzled, I stood there with my arms out in disbelief.

"Can't you see these people need help?" I yelled!

When another car that was approaching quickly stopped and turned around it dawned on me. I was covered with mud standing over a man bleeding profusely in the center of the highway with a rifle in my hand. That's not a good thing!

I ran back to the edge of the woods and hid my gun on the backside of a pine tree. Before I even got back up on the highway, cars were starting to stop and give assistance to the people in the two cars. I stood looking down at the man lying in the center of the highway, not knowing what I could do to help him and afraid to try.

The man stared back at me, glassy-eyed, with a puzzled look on his face like; "Why won't you help me?" A few people walked up and looked at him, then turned away, going back to help the people in the cars. Why wouldn't anyone help him? What should I do?

Traffic started backing up on the highway, and someone asked me to help direct the cars around the man lying there on the yellow line. An elderly lady was gawking at the cars in the ditches as she drove by and to my horror, drove over the poor man's arm. Blood gushed out his wound and sprayed me with red droplets. I fought not to throw up, but it was no use. My stomach churned and then turned upside down, and I lost it.

One of the men helping direct traffic saw me vomit and noticed my muddy clothes. "Were you thrown through the windshield?" He asked.

"No sir, I was just hunting in the woods. I heard the crash and was the first one here." He relieved me from directing traffic and suggested I should leave, as there were enough people helping. I left my gun in the woods and walked home in a daze that lasted the rest of the day.

Papaw went to Leesville the next day and heard that the man had died from loss of blood. I don't know if the lady driving over his arm killed him, but I'm sure it didn't help. It took a long time to get this out of my mind.

Each time I walked to Sandy Creek, the blood stains on the highway reminded me of the accident. The months passed quickly and the rains soon washed away all traces of the wreck, except what haunted my mind.

The next weekend I found an old abandoned dock on a slough off the upper reaches of Sandy Creek, and started leaving the pirogue there. It wasn't always there when I wanted to use it, but the boat's owner must have liked that place too, as he started returning it there and even took the chain and lock off. I'm sure he must have appreciated how well I took care of the boat. I guess it was just my dumb luck that we never met in person.

✦

Each day's activities centered on what Big Mama expected me to bring home for supper. If it was cold outside she called that Gumbo Weather. She could make gumbo out of almost anything and it always tasted fantastic. If she wanted a hog, which fortunately didn't happen often, it would consume most of a day. Just any hog wouldn't work. It had to be just the right size, and not an old razor back boar, as they were too tough to eat. I was proud that I was helping contribute to our food supply, but really dreaded dragging a hundred pound hog through the woods for a mile or more.

Wild razor back hogs ran with the domestic pigs in the woods behind our house, and anything that didn't have an ear tag was fair game according to Big Mama.

"We're getting low on hog headcheese," Big Mama would say, as she cleared the sink and prepared to butcher, even before I left the house. There was no discussing it. No asking if we could put it off until tomorrow, because I had planned to go fishing. It was like a chore, and I knew to put the fishing pole away and bring out the rifle. Big Mama bragged that we didn't throw anything away but the oink when we butchered a hog. Her idea of a seven course meal was a pound of hogshead cheese and a six pack of beer.

The flood plain of Sandy Creek was the best place to hunt pigs for several reasons. It was close to our house, so dragging a hog home wasn't as much work as it would have been if I hunted the other creeks. Also, the ground was littered with nuts, and the pigs always seemed to be there.

The greatest danger was a big razorback boar that ruled the pack. I tried to avoid him, but as I came up the creek bank, there he stood. We were both frozen in time, staring at each other. I was afraid to blink or even breathe for fear I would trigger a charge. Besides, my single shot rifle misfired about half the time.

We looked at each other for what seemed like five minutes, and then I cautiously moved off to the side, keeping my eyes on the hog. I'm sure if he had chosen to charge, the whole pack would have followed him, and I would have been in deep trouble.

I came across that old boar a few more times in the months to follow but always gave him all the respect my shaking legs would allow.

We had pork only when the weather was cooler; but our staple was armadillos. I think a lot of people in Louisiana and East

Texas would starve, were it not for the abundance of armadillos. Considered poor people food, most folks would never admit to eating it, but I've heard that during the Depression, President Hoover had considered feeding them to the country. Some people called them Hoover Hogs, Possums in a Half Shell and Texas Turkeys. It seemed like we practically lived on armadillos, corn bread and beans.

The good thing about armadillos was I didn't need to waste a bullet to bring home dinner. I would walk real slow and quiet through the woods about the time the sun was going down. I could hear armadillos rustling in the leaves for food.

Sneaking up on them is a real challenge because they have a keen sense of smell so they can detect a presence from a great distance. When they stand up on their hind legs, that's the clue to charge, as they know danger is close and they always run.

An armadillo can run at about the same speed as a person, only they take short cuts under bushes that we have to go around. Without fail, they dive into a hole and leave their tail visible. That's when the fun really starts.

I would run my hand down the hole and grab the armadillo's tail, just as close to its body as possible. You can't pull them out immediately, but if you hold on like your life depends on it, they eventually can be pulled back out.

The whole time I'd be pulling, the armadillo would dig its sharp claws into the sides of the hole and kick dirt all over me, along with a fire ant or two.

When I'd have the armadillo free of the hole and off the ground, it would be easy to cut its throat with a knife. I learned real quick to *never* hold an armadillo close to my body, or those sharp claws will open a person up.

After I had the armadillo home, Big Mama would have Papaw cut the armor off. After removing the meat, he would fasten the armadillo's head to its tail with wire, then hang it outside on the porch to use for flower baskets.

Big Mama reasoned that if we could sell the baskets, one armadillo should equal one pint of whisky with 25 cents left over. She said I could keep the change.

Chapter TWENTY-NINE

J ust a short distance down the hill from our house an older couple lived in a small home almost hidden from view by the trees. We shared the same driveway, and each day they stopped by our house when they walked to the highway to check their mail.

They were unquestionably a little backward, and maybe even a bit on the inquisitive side. Big Mama called it just plain nosey and really had a dislike for snooping neighbors. The man had one eye that looked off to the side when he talked. Big Mama nicknamed him, the old cock-eyed son-of-a-bitch. She was rather insulting to them on more than one occasion, but it didn't seem to matter much. In just a few days, they'd be stopping by our house again, just being neighborly, as they called it.

Maybe our neighbor's timing was always bad. If Big Mama was sober, her nerves would be on edge; company was the last thing she wanted. Of course if Big Mama was drunk, she just said what was on her mind and she didn't always have good thoughts. Probably the best time for visitors would be after she had a few drinks, but not yet fully intoxicated.

Big Mama suspected the neighbors snooped through our house when we weren't home. No one had locks on their doors. I'm not even certain we had doors on our house; I sure don't remember them ever being closed.

Big Mama told Papaw several times she thought canned goods were missing out of our pantry. But what really upset her more than the canned goods, was that this time our sausage was missing. Sausage was a major ingredient for Big Mama's gumbo and the main reason I didn't mind dragging a hundred pound pig for a mile.

We had just returned home from a liquor run when Big Mama discovered the sausage gone. About an hour later we noticed a car go down to the neighbor's house.

The neighbors didn't get many visitors, but about once a month the same car would show up and take them to town for their monthly supplies.

As the car drove back by our front porch, the neighbor lady was in the back seat, gawking out the window. The sight of her stare, sparked renewed anger in Big Mama. There sure was no doubt in Big Mama's mind who was stealing our food.

"What the hell are you looking at, you thieving bitch?" Big Mama shouted toward their car.

I doubt they could hear what Big Mama yelled, but their mouths hung open like they had read her lips. If they could have seen the anger on Big Mama's face, I'm sure they were able to tell what she was yelling at them.

As the afternoon passed, Big Mama wouldn't shut up about her stolen sausages and the old bitch down the hill.

To pass the afternoon, I decided to do a little target practicing. I positioned myself on my stomach in the shade of the front porch and started shooting beer cans I'd stacked in the yard. Papaw would cheer me on each time the bullet hit, causing the cans to fly. Soon the noise attracted Big Mama's attention, and she staggered out on our front porch.

"Cliff honey, why don't you take the rifle down to the neighbors and get us some chickens? That'll teach the nosy bitch to steal from us! I would rather use sausage for my gumbo, but I can damn sure double up on the chicken if I have to," she mumbled.

"Okay," I answered, almost surprised at what she wanted me to do. "How many should I kill?"

"Why don't you just kill 'em all?" Big Mama slurred as she staggered back in the house. "See if they have any green onions or peppers in their garden. I could use some of them, too. Here, just take a sack with you and load up."

"Looks like we're going to have chicken gumbo," I told Papaw as I stuck the box of .22 shells in my front pocket.

He shook his head side to side, and breathed out the familiar sigh I had heard many times before. Papaw knew better than to say anything. We both knew you don't argue with Big Mama when she's drinking, or there'd be hell to pay.

I could almost hear the music from some old gunslinger movie playing in my head, as I walked down the hill to the neighbor's house carrying my gun. I sure hoped they didn't come home while I was there.

A few chickens were scratching around in the dirt, and moved back to the far end of their pen when I opened the gate. Throwing the door open to the chicken house, I stood there letting my eyes adjust to the change in light. All the hens looked at me, clucking nervously, as a brave rooster came strutting across the floor like an elegant dressed warrior, ready to do battle.

I felt like I had a six shooter in each hand instead of a single shot .22 rifle. As I opened fire, the mean rooster was the first to die, but soon chickens and feathers were flying everywhere.

It was a bloody, brutal massacre. When the feathers had stopped falling and the cackling had quit, I didn't see any survivors. It was somewhat sad in a way, but Big Mama wanted chickens, and boy, did we have chickens.

Singing the Johnny Cash song to myself; *"Don't Take Your Guns To Town,"* I raided their garden and packed home all the chickens and fresh vegetables I could carry. Big Mama seemed pleased but Papaw was still shaking his head and mumbling profanities.

When the neighbors came home they rushed right up to our place very upset, and questioning what had happened. Big Mama said she saw a chicken hawk down there making quite a commotion, and she had sent me down with the rifle to kill it.

The man was curious if I had killed the hawk, so Big Mama called me out from my hiding in the bedroom. "Cliff, were you able to kill that chicken hawk?" She asked.

"Um— not with the first shot but I did kill it," I lied, watching the expression on Big Mama's face for her approval.

The neighbor thanked me, and said he only had three chickens left alive. Big Mama gave me a look from hell like; Didn't I tell you to kill 'em all?

The neighbor was almost out of our yard when he stopped and turned around. "Listen, I've got chickens scattered all over my yard, and they're just going to waste away in this hot sun. Would y'all like a few?"

Big Mama through her head back and in her most sarcastic voice said; "No thank you, we only eat *fresh* meat. Now if you'll excuse me, I'm going back inside for my afternoon tea."

With her chin in the air, she strutted back inside with all the class of a southern high society southern lady.

CHAPTER
THIRTY

Hunting had become my everyday life. Not only did I enjoy the exploring part of going deep into the piney woods, but it gave me a reason to get out of the house and freedom to ponder my life, with no outside interference.

One of my most embarrassing hunting trips happened on opening day of squirrel season. I never had a license to hunt and would shoot almost anything that was edible. The only way I knew a hunting season had opened was when I met other hunters in the woods. On this day I was walking along an old logging road when I met a jeep with Texas license plates. Three men in the jeep stopped and asked me where the best places were to hunt. I pointed them to the direction of Sandy Creek and warned them to be sure and watch out for the razorback bore.

After providing them with all I knew about the area, I continued on down the road toward home. It wasn't long before I spotted a squirrel, lying on a stump sunning itself. He hadn't seen me and a quick shot with my .22 rifle knocked him off on the ground.

I had just hung the squirrel from my belt and walked about fifteen minutes when I heard the jeep coming back up the logging road toward me. I moved out of the way so they could pass but instead they stopped beside me as their dust settled.

"Did you have any luck," I asked awkwardly.

I wasn't accustom to communicate with other people, especially in *my* woods. My old "you're trespassing" instincts were surfacing.

"No, we didn't see a thing. I think your Sandy Creek is squirreled out," one of the men laughed as he popped the top on a can of Jax beer.

"How about you, did you get anything?" one of the men asked.

Proudly, I pulled the trophy sized squirrel from my belt and held it up for them to inspect. They asked me where I got it and when I told them I shot it off a stump as it was sunning itself, they all busted out laughing. One of the men said he had shot it himself and planned to pick it up when they were driving back past it. I was so embarrassed my face had to be as red as a Louisiana sunset after a forest fire. I tried to give it back to them but they were all laughing hysterically as they pulled away leaving me in the dust.

I was too embarrassed to tell Big Mama and Papaw where that squirrel came from. We had squirrel gumbo for supper that night, and it was delicious no matter how I came by it.

We were surprised one warm summer night when Morris, Mom and Rocky showed up. I couldn't believe that Mom had been released from prison so soon, but was afraid to ask questions.

Big Mama and Papaw were between paychecks but Morris and Mom had money and soon the four of them were all drinking. That surprised me too, because I had never seen Mom drink beer. Mom seemed to be keeping everyone in control and insisted they were going to stick to beer. No hard liquor!

Mom said they were going to stay with us until they could get on their feet and find work. She promised when they had the money, she would rent a house and I could move in with them. I wasn't sure I liked that plan, as I worried about losing my freedom and still had bad memories from living with her before. And what if they found a house in town? I would hate that.

Mom started looking for employment in Leesville, but her rap sheet was longer than her job résumé. The only employment she could find was a job working at a bar. It surprised me that she would work there, since she didn't like being around drunks.

Mom starting putting in a lot of hours and would come home to find Morris, Big Mama and Papaw all drunk. Of course that led to nightly arguments.

Big Mama and Papaw were in bed one night when Mom came home. Morris had been drinking most of the day and it turned into yet another argument.

"Morris, you don't know how hard I work all day, and then come home to this. How are we ever going to save enough money to rent our own place if you drink it all away? Have you even looked for a job today?" Mom cried.

Morris jumped to his feet and hit Mom in the face, knocking her down on the couch. He packed his things and left with the car. If Big Mama or Papaw had seen it happen, Morris' life would have most likely ended that night. There's no doubt Big Mama would have killed him if she had the chance.

A few nights later Rocky and I were out walking and discovered Morris hiding in the woods near the house. He grabbed Rocky and ran with him to where his car was hidden on an old logging road. I stood there in shock, not knowing what to do.

Morris knew better than to come to the house, as Big Mama would have shot him. In fact, she was mad at me for not doing it myself when I had the chance, as I had my .22 rifle with me.

Grabbing the rifle away from me, she fired wild, random shots toward the woods, not even knowing if Morris was still there. I reminded her that Rocky was with him and she may shoot him by accident.

"Your right, the worthless bastard is probably using him for a human shield!" she screamed.

For the next few hours she paced back and forth on the front porch with the gun in her hands, stopping occasionally for another drink. I'm sure Morris was miles into Texas and had no intention of coming back, but she maintained a faithful watch just in case he should return.

❧

With no transportation, Mom was forced to stay in Leesville in the back of the bar where she worked. Several times a week, Papaw would make liquor runs into Leesville and if Mom wasn't busy, we would have lunch with her.

We were surprised when we stopped by the bar to see Mom one afternoon and she wasn't there. The owner of the bar took Papaw aside and said that the police had arrested her for a bad check. As far as he knew, she was in the Vernon Parish Jail.

On the drive across town to the jail, Papaw kept mumbling; "I can't believe that she is still writing checks. When in the hell is she going to learn she can't get away with that shit?"

"Would you just shut the hell up and drive Mr. Perfect? I wouldn't be a damn bit surprised if Morris made the call that got her caught. It would be just like the worthless bastard to do that," Big Mama cursed.

We went to see Mom and were escorted by a deputy sheriff up the stairs to the jail. The sound of those big metal doors closing behind us made my stomach turn. It's the sound of freedom lost, and nothing on this earth sounds like a jail door closing behind you. The air was hot and thick with the smell of stale cigarettes. I hated being there.

The deputy left us alone to talk. Mom whispered she had a big secret she wanted to share with us. She had escaped from prison in Lansing, Kansas. That didn't really surprise me or Big

Mama. Mom didn't think the local sheriff knew about the escape yet since he hadn't said anything about Kansas. She explained that if the sheriff found out, they would extradite her back to Kansas and she would probably be there the rest of her life.

I was curious how she escaped from the prison and just had to ask. Visions of guns blazing, the wail of a distant siren in the middle of the night and a fast getaway car filled my mind. Mom ruined the mental picture when she said they just forgot to lock her door one night and she just walked away. I knew she had to be kidding, but it was obvious she wasn't going to tell me the truth.

"I've got some very serious things to discuss with you both," Mom whispered. "Cliff, I think you're old enough to understand, so I'm going to give it to you straight. I need to have another escape plan ready in case Kansas finds out I'm here."

"What can we do to help?" Big Mama asked with a puzzled look.

"Well, here's my plan for now. If Kansas doesn't find out I'm here, I'll just stay in jail and see what kind of sentence the judge gives me on the check charge. The check was only written for $35.00, and it's an old one from when I was here before. If you could make restitution, I think the judge will give me probation. That is, unless he finds out about Kansas. If that happens, he'll throw the book at me, and I'll probably go to the woman's prison in Angola. When I've done my time there, Kansas will most likely want me. Believe me, I don't want to go to Angola, or back to Lansing."

"Mom, I just had an idea where you can go if you decide to

escape." Both she and Big Mama looked at me as if they were open to suggestions.

"I have a pirogue hidden in an abandoned boat shed up Sandy Creek. The boat is big enough to hold two people, and I could be waiting under the highway bridge for you when you escape. The shed doesn't have any walls, but I bet Papaw and I could build some. I could bring you food each day and no one would ever find you."

"You know for a 12 year old boy you're pretty smart, but I'm not going to live in the woods in a boat shed the rest of my life," Mom laughed.

"We could take the pirogue down Anacoco Bayou to the Sabine River, and then go all the way to Orange. You said your friend Corinne moved there. I bet she would help you again. I could catch fish for supper and we could camp on the sandbars at night. It would be a lot of fun," I told Mom beaming with excitement.

"I'm sure it would son, but I've already got my own plan and yes, you can help. You can start by coming to visit me every-day. Every time you come, bring two or three Hershey bars with you."

Big Mama and I both looked at Mom like she had lost her mind.

"Okay—but I don't understand how that will help," Big Mama frowned.

"I want Cliff to carry the candy bars to see if the jailer checks them. It will be a test."

"I get it—you want me to sneak in a gun!" Now Mom's plan was starting to make sense.

"No, just wait! I'll tell you when you need to know when its time, and there won't be any guns."

We made our first trial run the next day. Big Mama brought a sack with a few items that Mom needed, and I carried three Hershey bars. The jailer looked through Big Mama's bag before allowing us into the jail, but only glanced at the candy bars in my hand.

The next day was a repeat of the first, as well as all the other days that week. The jailer would look through anything that Big Mama carried, but he never gave my candy bars a second glance.

With the trial runs out of the way, it was time for the real thing. Big Mama broke hacksaw blades so that they were slightly smaller than a Hershey bar.

Carefully, she heated the broken blades and then placed then on the back of the Hershey bars and watched as they melted the chocolate. Using the heated blade of a butter knife, she gently pushed the hacksaw blade into the melted chocolate, so that the hacksaw blades were hidden inside. Ever so carefully, she smoothed the bottom of the chocolate bar as it hardened and then slipped the wrapper back on. You couldn't even tell it had been tampered with.

"Cliff, if the jailer pulls the wrapper off and notices the chocolates been melted, just tell him you laid the candy on the car dash and the sun melted it. Don't be nervous about it. I don't think he will even check."

That next Sunday was the big day we planned to deliver the hacksaw blades. Mom said Sunday would be the best, as the jail would be crowded with visitors, and the jailer would be in a hurry to get people in and out. He wouldn't be as likely to notice if we were a little bit nervous.

I was awake early Sunday morning and heard a flock of geese fly low over the house honking. They disappeared out of sight, just over the pine trees and landed in Anacoco Lake. If this had happened any other day, we would be having goose for supper, but today we had a mission.

I thought about Mom pacing back and forth in her small cell, knowing we would soon arrive with her keys to freedom. I couldn't help but wonder what her plans were after she broke out. Would she come by the house and get me? Would she go to Colorado where Morris and Rocky probably were?

Big Mama woke up a pint low. A stiff drink of whiskey for breakfast calmed her shaking hands. When we arrived at the court house she tilted the bottle up and had another five gurgle drink in the parking lot before we went inside.

I carried the Hershey Bars in one hand and avoided looking at them for fear it would give the secret away. The deputy glanced toward my hand but didn't say anything. He checked Big Mama's purse and bags before letting us in. As we walked up the stairs to the jail I became so tense, I'm surprised the Hershey bars didn't melt in my hand.

Mom had a bright smile as I reached through the cell bars and handed her the Hershey's. After she had the hacksaw blades hidden in a hole in her mattress, she readied us for the next part of her well calculated plan.

Mom told Big Mama to go to the thrift stores and buy a ceramic angel figurine. "If they don't have one, find a ceramic store. I know they have them. If you can't find one around here, drive to Houston if you have to. This is very important. It has to be an angel that's breakable, nothing else would work. And one more thing, a gray angel would be best." Mom demanded.

When we left the jail, Papaw drove Big Mama and me all over Leesville. I ran in the stores and checked for ceramic angels, while Big Mama and Papaw stayed in the truck and drank. I couldn't find one anywhere in town, so we drove to DeRidder. At a pawn shop I found a cream colored angel about 7" tall that Big Mama said would be just right. She handed me the $4.00 that it was priced at, and I rushed back in and bought it.

It took a lot of fast talking between Mom and Big Mama to talk the jailer into letting Mom have the angel in her cell. It was strictly for religious reasons, they assured him.

Just as planned, Mom broke the angel statue a few days later. She cried like her own heart was shattered. After all, the angel had been in the family for such a long time. Mom explained to the jailer between her sobs, that dying family members had held the angel as they passed to the other side. How could she ever tell her grandmother it was broken? Mom could talk anyone into almost anything. With a few more tears she had the jailer talked into letting Big Mama bring her some paint and glue to make the repairs.

Working at night, mom had the bars in her door cut out in no time, and glued back into place. Using the paint intended for the broken angel, she painted the cuts she had made on the bars to match their original colors.

It's impossible to cut your way out of a jail, without the other prisoners knowing about it. Soon word spread throughout the jail and most of the men awaiting sentencing decided they wanted to escape too. The used hacksaw blades and paint were passed around the jail as more prisoners planned their escape to freedom.

As the numbers wanting to escape increased, so did the offers for assistance. One of the men said his wife had a station wagon and she would help with the getaway. Another knew of a place out of state they could all hide until things cooled off, while another had enough money to pay for their travel expenses.

As the size of the escape plan grew, so did Big Mama's apprehension. Our visits were purposely cut back to only once each week, so if a jailbreak did happen, no one would suspect we had a part in it.

One of the men knew he was going to the state penitentiary and didn't want to wait for the judge and sentencing. Against the others wishes he escaped a few days ahead of time. That brought pressure down on those who remained.

The next morning, the sheriff and his deputies were banging on the bars with a sledge hammer as the jail fell apart before their unbelieving eyes. When they checked Mom's cell, amazingly they didn't find any bars that had been cut.

All the men were immediately rushed to other jails in the adjoining cities and parishes. Only Mom remained in Leesville.

The very next day Mom went to court for sentencing. Big Mama, Papaw and I all sat on the third row of the hard wooden seats with our fingers crossed.

Our hearts sunk and Mom lay her head down on the oak

table in front of her, and sobbed. The judge told her that Kansas had contacted the Louisiana authorities, and they planned to extradite her after she served her time in Louisiana. The judge sentenced Mom to the maximum term possible, to be served in the penitentiary in Angola, Louisiana.

We knew that Mom would go ahead with her escape plan but now she wouldn't have the help of the men in the jail. Big Mama leaned over and whispered in my ear, with breath that would have knocked a buzzard off a meat wagon.

"Cliff, it's up to us now. No one else is going to help her."

After we left the courthouse, we waited on the lawn outside the jail hoping we could talk to Mom before they locked her up again. The jailer was leading her in handcuffs back to her cell when we approached. He informed us if we wanted to visit we would have to wait about half an hour.

Even outside the building we heard the heavy metal door slam shut. A male voice immediately started cussing, and strangely Mom started singing the first few lines to the Hank Locklin song, *"Please Help Me I'm Falling"* over and over. It was easy to see something was going on, but I wasn't sure what.

When learned later that when the jailer returned Mom to her cell, the bars in her door fell out on the floor!

When the jail staff checked Mom's cell after the escape, they had hit all the bars with the sledgehammer. Everything was secure. How could this happen now?

It seems they overlooked one important area. They had failed to check the bars on the open cell door!

Big Mama grabbed my hand in a death grip, and practically dragged me across the court house lawn to our car. She kept glancing anxiously into the rear view mirror all the way home, just knowing the sheriff would come up behind us at anytime.

We didn't get to see Mom again, nor did we try. She was transported to the woman's prison that afternoon.

CHAPTER

THIRTY-TWO

When the summer ended I started school in Evans, Louisiana. Big Mama warned me not to wear shoes to school because, as she put it, "All the kids will think you're rich and tease you."

"You're in Louisiana now son and everyone is poor. Don't be making fun of the other kids," she warned. For some reason, I didn't feel like we were rich. I would be the last one to ever make fun of anyone for being poor.

When I caught the school bus that morning, I wanted to make myself invisible. I was the *only* kid on the bus without shoes. Every head followed me as I boarded and took a seat in the back. I was so mad at Big Mama. Was it because we didn't have the money or was she just being mean? Did she really believe none of the other kids would have shoes?

Everyone at school had shoes too. From the teasing I was getting, I knew it was going to be a long year. To say I was beginning to hate school would be an understatement.

Of course I wore shoes from that day on, and soon the teasing stopped. Eventually I started to fit in with the other kids.

I'm not sure what brought about the change, but Grandma sold her house in Bridge City and came to live with us. Big Mama was her daughter, but they were as opposite as night and day. Grandma had devoted her life to the Lord and it seemed odd for her to leave her friends and church behind to come live with us. None the less, it was a welcome change for me. Big Mama seemed to be annoyed at her coming to live with us and I didn't understand why. After all, she was a dear, sweet lady.

Grandma knew that Big Mama had a drinking problem, but it wasn't until she arrived that she witnessed how bad it had become. At the first opportunity, Grandma pulled me aside and asked how long Big Mama had been drinking this way.

"As long as I can remember," I answered truthfully.

"No, she didn't seem this bad when they lived on Sabine Lake or in Orange. Something is very wrong with her. You haven't seen the change?" she asked.

"No Ma'am, she was even drinking like this when we lived in Arkansas," I answered.

Grandma just sat down at the table with her Bible and started praying. I could feel a storm cloud brewing in our home, but I had no control over it. When Big Mama and Papaw came home from town, I silently prayed that Grandma wouldn't say anything about their drinking. Grandma retreated to the bedroom and stayed there reading the Bible until bedtime.

The next morning when the sun rose over the pine trees everything seemed fine. I hurried to get dressed and rushed out to catch the school bus.

All day my thoughts were on Grandma. I worried she was going to say the wrong thing to Big Mama. If she did, anything could happen. I think I knew Big Mama's explosive temperament better than anyone.

When the school bell rang, ending another day, the feeling that something was wrong grew even stronger.

Our house was fourteen miles from school, but I could see a column of smoke in the distance as the bus snaked its way toward Anacoco Lake. Fighting off the odd feeling, I tried to convince myself that it was probably a forest fire or someone burning slash. The closer the bus came to home, the larger the plume of smoke became.

When the bus stopped to let me off, I froze at the bottom of the steps. Big Mama was in her nightgown sitting in the ditch, too drunk to even stand without support.

Every kid on the school bus was crowded to the windows with their mouths open looking. I was embarrassed beyond words and so angry; I couldn't hold back the tears. Why did she have to do this to me? I was having a hard enough time at school without everyone seeing this. Why didn't the bus driver close the door and just drive away? He seemed to be just as curious as all the kids on the bus. I ignored the laughter flowing from the open windows and asked Big Mama what she was doing.

"What the hell does it look like? I burned the son-of-a-bitch down," she answered, pointing up the hill toward where our house had been. Her speech was heavily slurred, as she fought to keep her balance.

I just stood there numb, fighting the urge to strike out. The tears were running down my cheeks, and I wiped them off with my shirt sleeves. Big Mama was mumbling something else, but it was all gibberish.

I took a deep breath and walked on past her up the hill to where Grandma stood crying.

"Are you okay?" I asked, noticing she had a bad burn on one arm that had blistered. The sight made me nauseous.

"Grandma, what are we going to do?" I asked, still crying and fighting to clear the lump that was hanging in my throat.

"I know that God will find a way. He never gives us more than we can carry," she answered, wiping tears from her eyes.

I'm sure she wished she was still in Bridge City.

A cloud of dust settled in the driveway as Papaw jumped out of his car. He too, was in a state of shock. He walked around cussing, kicking the hot coals, and shaking his head in disbelief. It's probably a good thing Big Mama was still in the ditch down by the highway.

Papaw was furious when I told him that Big Mama said she started the fire. He just didn't want to believe it, and asked Grandma what had happened. As she went back over the day's events in detail as Papaw and I stood there listening. "She started drinking heavy this afternoon right after you left."

"Damn her hide," Papaw interrupted. "I told her when I left I'd be back in a few hours. I knew she was mad, but I promised a friend I'd help him pull a load of pine stumps."

"She really became angry when the mail lady dropped off a package for me," Grandma continued. "Some of my church friends in Bridge City sent me a nice nightgown. She became jealous and started cussing me out. Saying things like, *"You think you're better than me, don't you? You and your uppity church friends!"* I didn't know what to say. I told her that I didn't feel that way at all. When I started crying, she slapped me, knocking my glasses off. I didn't know what to do, so I went to my room to get away from her."

"What in the hell am I going to do with her?" Papaw cursed.

"About half an hour later, I could still hear her moving around in the other room," Grandma continued. "I thought it best to just stay away from her, so I laid down for a nap. I was almost asleep when I heard the bedroom door squeak open. I kept my eyes closed and pretended to be sleeping, hoping she would leave me alone. She walked on past my bed, and I saw her open the closet door. I closed my eyes again when she walked back past my bed and quietly closed the bedroom door behind her. I couldn't help but wonder what she was doing in the closet so I went to investigate. My new nightgown was lying on the floor—on fire!"

"Goddamn her," Papaw moaned. "What the hell was she thinking? I don't know what to do with her."

"I stomped the fire out," Grandma added; "and then lay back down to finish my nap. I'm not sure how long I slept, but when I awoke, the room was ablaze."

"My God, she tried to kill you!" Papaw groaned in grief.

"The good Lord was with me. I could never have escaped that inferno on my own." Grandma said, remaining strong in her beliefs. "The house was soon totally engulfed. Cliff, I tried to save your rabbits from their cage, but I couldn't get close because of the intense heat. I'm sorry, son; there was just nothing I could do."

"My rabbits—Son-of-a-bitch!"

"Cliff, you watch your language. I know you're upset, but I raised you better than that."

"I'm sorry Grandma, but sometimes she just makes me so mad. I'm just glad you made it out. I can't believe she did this to us." I gave her a hug that we both desperately needed.

Papaw and I both stood there surveying the damage. The sight made me sick. A large cedar tree that stood beside the house had disappeared except for a few burnt branches. All our clothes were gone. The mattress had burned away, leaving nothing but rust colored coil springs. A chunk of deformed plastic lay twisted where the radio had been. I kicked at the hot clumps looking for my rifle. All of Papaw's World War Two medals were gone and could never be replaced. The lawn mower that had been under the front porch sat with the rubber tires melted and burned away; the gas tank was still smoking.

"How could she do this?" I asked out loud. No one answered.

What bothered me most were my pet rabbits. Their fur was burned off and even their flesh was smoking. I thought of how they must have felt, being trapped in their cage with no way to escape. Big Mama needed a boot planted in her butt. There were no fire trucks, no police cars, no one around but our nosey neighbors from down the hill.

A shiny black car sped up the driveway, and slid to a stop in a cloud of dust right next to where we were standing. Big Mama had just staggered back up the drive as the landlady jumped out of the car. I could tell she was fighting mad when she stormed up to Big Mama. "What happened here?" she demanded.

It wasn't a good time to talk to Big Mama. I already knew what she was going to say before she even opened her mouth.

"What the hell does it look like? I burned the son-of-a-bitch down!"

"You did what?" The landlady demanded. Her mouth was open in disbelief.

"You heard me. I burned the son-of-a-bitch down!"

If there's such a thing as forty shades of red, the landlady's face went through every one of them. She marched back to her car, jumped in, spun a 180 degree circle in the dirt and headed down our drive toward the highway. Her tires squealed and gave off a puff of smoke as she reached the pavement and turned toward Leesville. She must have been doing 80 miles per hour before she reached the Sandy Creek Bridge.

It didn't seem like the landlady had been gone long before she pulled back in the driveway with two deputy sheriff's cars behind her. The deputies walked up to Big Mama with the land-lady marching beside them.

"You tell them—you tell them what you told me," the land-lady said almost stuttering.

I expected Big Mama to say the same thing again when she opened her mouth, but instead there was a hesitation. She took a deep breath and slowly began to speak; "I told her and told her she better get something done about the wiring in that house, but no, she just wouldn't listen. Are you happy now?" she asked, directing her question to the landlady.

Talk about mad, the landlady's face turned beet red all the way down to her neck, and her body started trembling. She stood there dumbfounded, shocked and totally exasperated with Big Mama's lies.

"Have you been drinking?" one of the deputies asked Big Mama.

Gee, where would he get an idea like that? I thought to myself.

"Yes I have officer, and I bet you would too if you lost everything you owned," Big Mama answered uninhibited by his question.

"Well this lady told us you admitted to setting the house on fire," the deputy said. "Did you have anything to do with this?"

"Do you really think I'd burn the house down and leave everything I own in it?" Big Mama asked, looking at the deputy like he was stupid. "I may have had a little to drink, but I'm not crazy. Now you better get that stupid bitch out of here before I slap the shit out of her for accusing me."

The deputies just shook their heads in disgust and walked off talking between themselves. The landlady assured Big Mama that this wasn't over yet, and added; "I'll see you in court!"

After kicking through the smoldering rubble and not finding anything that could be salvaged, all we could do was leave. The four of us climbed into the car with only the clothes on our backs.

Papaw started driving west on the highway toward Evans. Big Mama was in the front seat, and Grandma and I in the back. Papaw glanced toward Big Mama and asked; "Why did you do this?"

She sat there in silence for a moment and answered; "Well, you know how I always wanted a fireplace?" Big Mama still had a glazed look in her eyes but she had our full attention. "I took some of those old fence posts that were piled in the backyard and carried them into the house. I laid two on the floor in this direction, and then two the other direction, and just kept stacking them higher and higher. Then I took a grocery sack and started a fire in the center."

Before Big Mama could finish what she was saying, Papaw reached across the car and backhanded her across the face. Her head bounced off the seat and then fell against the side window with a thud. She was either unconscious or smart enough to pretend that she was.

I don't believe in hitting a woman, but if anyone ever deserved to be smacked—she did. It would have suited me just fine if Papaw would have pulled over and left Big Mama in the ditch.

CHAPTER
THIRTY-THREE

The fire totally disrupted our lives. Everything we owned was gone and there was no money to replace anything. There was no Red Cross or Salvation Army offering us a place to stay. No offers of clothes to replace what we had lost. We were on our own, with nowhere to go. I can't blame the service groups for not helping, as I doubt they could have found us if they tried.

Our helping hand came from an old trapper named Charlie who lived alone in a small cabin just a few miles north of Evans. Charlie loaned Papaw a tent and offered to let me stay with him until we found a place to live, but only if I would agree to help him run his trap line each day. Of course I readily agreed to his generous offer. It was a professional relationship that turned into friendship.

Grandma Nora moved to Sweeny, Texas to live with Aunt Gwen and Uncle Willie. Big Mama and Papaw chose a sandbar overlooking Anacoco Bayou for their campsite. They could have just pitched the tent in Charlie's yard, but the bayou offered them privacy and was closer to the bootlegger in Merryville.

Charlie's cabin was made of logs that were weathered from the years of Louisiana storms. The walls were covered with the tanned hides of bobcats, raccoons, fox and possum. His few possessions consisted of various traps, some odd pieces of clothing, a few pots and a skillet. A shotgun and a rifle hung on the wall. All he owned and needed in his world was there, and I could tell he was content with that.

Charlie's cabin was dark inside but had a fireplace along one wall that would light up the room at night. A white-tailed deer hide graced the floor in front of the fireplace. The nightly fires made the cabin warm and welcome. We would sit by the fire's eerie orange glow, basking in the warmth of a crackling fire, while Charlie told me hunting and fishing stories from his own childhood. The dictionary would run out of words before Charlie ran out of stories. We had a strong connection. Staring at the shadows of the flickering light until the hot coals were gone, I'd fall asleep on a pallet in front of the fireplace.

I was grateful to Charlie for taking me in and wished I could just stay with him full time. I started calling him Uncle Charlie and wondered if there was someway he could adopt me. I wondered if he had similar feelings, but I was afraid to ask him. It would have probably been better if I had told people how I felt during some of the situations I had been through. Instead I had learned to keep my feelings and thoughts to myself. I tried hard not to show my heart to anyone. After all, a heart can be very vulnerable.

It didn't matter if it was pouring down rain or not, Uncle Charlie and I would go out in the storm early in the morning and check those traps. It was often bone chilling cold, but I didn't mind. It was important to gain his respect and I tried to act older than I was, so he would depend on me more. After we got back to his cabin he would start skinning out whatever we had caught (raccoons, bobcats etc.) while I got ready for school.

I was embarrassed to even go to school because most of the kids knew about the fire, and the rumors had circulated about Big Mama being drunk in the ditch.

I didn't have much to wear except a few extra clothes that Uncle Charlie had found. I'm sure I didn't smell the best either after we finished trapping and skinning animals. Uncle Charlie didn't have anything other than the kitchen sink to clean up in. I'm not sure how long it had been since I had a real bath. After being teased on the bus a few times about Big Mama, I started walking to and from school each day.

Tears would form in my eyes when the school bus passed and a few kids would yell out names. I couldn't stand the pain as it grew inside me each day. I felt as if I would surely explode. After the name calling happened a few times, I started looking over my shoulder watching for the school buses. When I saw them approaching, I would hurry into the woods at the highway's edge, just out of sight, until after they passed. Only then would I continue walking to Uncle Charlie's.

Monday arrived with the sound of thunder, and we awoke to a heavy rain. The trees offered some relief from the downpour as we hurried to empty the traps and reset them for another day. I probably should have ridden the bus, because I was sopping wet before I arrived at school. At least no one could say I hadn't had a bath.

I noticed the teacher watching me, and then she left the room for a few minutes. Shortly after she returned to my classroom, the principal called me into his office. Looking at me in an inquiring manner, he wanted to know why I was walking and not riding the bus. Evidently someone had seen me duck into the bushes. After I explained why, he called the bus driver in for a meeting. I was embarrassed to even discuss this with them. I'm sure a lot of my problem was just my low self esteem. Even someone's stare would cause me embarrassment.

The principal and bus driver assured me that they would talk to the other kids about teasing me if I wanted them to. What I wanted was for everyone, including the principal and bus driver, to just leave me alone.

After a lot of talking on their part, I agreed to start riding the bus again. Just a few days after the meeting with the principal, someone from the school dropped off a box of clothes at Uncle Charlie's.

A few months went by, and I started to come out of my shell and made a few friends at school. It was Friday with only an hour of school remaining when it happened. Uncle Charlie had cooked beans the day before, and I could feel movement within my digestive system. The longer I held it in, the larger I could feel it grow. I tried to slip out a nice quiet fart, but instead, it came out much like a small explosion in the back of the classroom where I was sitting. With all the prior teasing I had been getting, that's all I needed. Each and every head in the class room turned to see who let one, and I just couldn't help myself. If it had still been storming outside, I could have passed it off as thunder. Instead, I pointed at the kid in front of me and started laughing too. He looked up and saw the kids laughing and then turned around just in time to see me pointing toward him. "It wasn't me!" he shouted. "I didn't do it!" He fired an angry glare toward me with hate written all over his face, and I knew

I was in deep trouble.

From that day on it was a persistent contest of survival. At recess I kept an eye on where he was and made sure I had time to reach the classroom if he started after me. After school I would make a mad dash to the school bus and always sit in the front seat near the driver. He even got off at my bus stop, miles from where he lived in an attempt to pound me. I was faster than he was and hit the ground running.

We were all in the sixth grade, and he was three times my size. It seemed like even the teacher was afraid of him. At recess he would smoke cigarettes on the playground. If a teacher said anything that made him mad, he would walk over to the highway and start hitchhiking. Now that's definitely ditching in the first degree. On a field trip to Leesville, he just walked away and wasn't back when we were ready to leave on the bus, so the teachers just left him behind. After the fart incident, I spent the rest of the school year running but he never caught me. He probably even forgot why he was chasing me after a few weeks had passed. Kind of a conditioned response; if I ran, he chased.

Big Mama and Papaw didn't come by Uncle Charlie's for a long time, and I wondered if they were in jail somewhere. Just when I thought they had forgotten about me and I could live happily ever after with Uncle Charlie, they showed up one day and said we were moving to Texas.

"But Big Mama, I thought you hated Texas," I said with a

tone suggesting that maybe she forgot.

"This is a different part of Texas than you've ever seen before. I think it's going to be a lot better than Bridge City," Big Mama answered with enthusiasm; "Your Aunt Gwen, Uncle Willie, Grandma and all your cousins are living in Sweeny. It will be nice to be close to family again." I wondered how Uncle Willie would feel about us moving there, as he despised their drinking.

Big Mama's decision to move was most likely influenced from fear of being prosecuted for arson. She hated the Leesville jail as much as Mom did, and I'm sure getting arrested was heavy on her mind.

It was hard to tell Uncle Charlie goodbye, but I didn't have a choice. He had a tear in the corner of his eye when I thanked him for letting me stay there. As I reached out and shook his hand goodbye, he pulled me close and gave me a hug. But like many relationships, it ended abruptly. We had filled a void in each others' lives. I never saw Uncle Charlie again after that day.

Within an hour we had crossed the bridge over the Sabine River and stopped at a drive-in restaurant in Burkeville, Texas. I ran inside and ordered three hamburgers to go, while Big Mama and Papaw waited in the car. The girl behind the counter had the deepest blue eyes that twinkled, and a smile that made my legs shaky. I was in love, but unfortunately we were just passing through. In no time we were deep in the piney woods of East Texas.

We passed through Jasper without stopping or even seeing a police car. Driving back roads, Papaw stayed off the main highways as much as possible. He drove miles out of the way to avoid Houston and late the next day, we arrived at our destination: Sweeny, Texas.

CHAPTER

THIRTY-FOUR

As much as I hated it, I was forced to attend yet another new school. I had just turned fourteen, and this was the seventh school I had attended since the first grade. The teacher in Sweeny did something that should be made mandatory at all schools. She introduced me to the class, telling them what she knew about me and where I was from. Then to top off my welcome, she assigned a student to show me around. My guide was a boy named Tommy Brooks who seemed to be one of the more popular kids in the class. We became friends and started hanging out together. If the teacher hadn't made this arrangement, I'm sure I would have found a place to hide in the back of the class. Most likely I would have found other kids like myself, the wrong side of the river type. From past experiences I had become a battle-scarred loner, but Tommy helped to change that. At that age trouble is knocking on the door, and I could have easily gone either way.

Sweeny was different than anywhere we had lived in a number of ways. I was amazed by the large jungle like plants called Palmetto that grew in the woods behind our house. If you were dropped off there blind folded, you would have sworn you were in Africa or deep in the Amazon jungle. Hurricane Carla had just hit the area, blowing over huge trees everywhere. Their roots were pulled out of the ground, making huge walls of dirt for my cousins and me to climb on. We would pretend we were high in the mountains, climbing cliffs that dropped hundreds of feet below us.

With miles of forest to explore, I found a large pond surrounded by a swamp near the San Bernard River. I had talked Papaw into buying me a .22 rifle to replace the one we lost in the fire, with the promise of ducks for supper. There was so much brush around the pond that it was hard to see the open water without going out in a boat.

It wasn't long before I had water up to my chest. I moved slowly and quietly as I could to reach the ducks without scaring them off.

As I approached the open water, I saw four ducks sitting across the pond. Carefully, I aimed my gun, but just as I was about to squeeze the trigger, something came up under the ducks and scared them off. It looked like the bottom had boiled up, like a giant gas bubble. I had heard of that happening but had never witnessed it with my own eyes.

As I stood there watching in amazement, the bubble started moving toward me. By the time it was halfway to me, I started looking for a tree to climb.

Shimmying up a small willow tree about one foot thick, I rested with one foot in a fork in the branches, just five feet above the water. From my perch in the tree it was plain to see, a huge alligator was coming right toward me. It swam right to where I had been standing and stopped, as if it were studying the mud that I had stirred up in the water. Slowly, it turned and put its nose right up against the tree I was in. I noticed my weight was causing the tree to sway back and forth and the alligator seemed to be watching the ripples in the water.

I thought about shooting the alligator, but what if he saw me move and he knocked me out of the tree with his tail? Then the thought occurred to me that the .22 caliber bullet may just make it mad. I could visualize the alligator thrashing around, turning the water bloody and attracting even more alligators. I decided that doing nothing but hanging on for my life was my best option.

Almost as quickly as the alligator arrived, it swam off across the pond and disappeared into the swamp. I jumped down from the tree and took off in the opposite direction as fast as I could move through the water, to the safety of the shore.

As the story about my experience with the alligator spread around school, added to the fact I had moved to Sweeny from Louisiana (known for its alligator population), I became "the local alligator expert."

My popularity at school grew, and my grades started moving up without the need for me to make changes to my report card myself. The only thing that hadn't changed was my home life. I just never knew what condition Big Mama and Papaw would be in, so I couldn't take a chance and bring friends home. My friends would invite me to spend the night at their house, but I never reciprocated.

Each weekend I'd be back at the pond looking for the alligator, or exploring the San Bernard River, usually with friends looking for an adventure. On one such occasion, I promised my friends I would show them an alligator if they could borrow a boat. One of the boys had a homemade rowboat, and his dad hauled it to the pond for us.

The boat was a little overloaded with four of us in it. The gunnels were so low that the water was just a few inches flooding the boat. It would have been no big deal if that had happened, except for getting my gun wet and the possibility of an alligator encounter while swimming.

We were in the center of the pond when one of my friends spotted something moving rapidly toward us from out of the cattails.

"Hurry, Cliff, It's going to attack!" one of my friends yelled. Looking down the open sights, I followed the movement in the water until it was in close range. As I opened fire, the creature dove below the surface so I couldn't tell if the bullet had hit its target.

We were afraid the alligator would come up under our boat, or worse yet just come over the side and grab one of us. My crew was divided. Two of the boys thought we should grab the paddles and row, while Tommy thought I should just keep shooting down into the water toward where it had disappeared.

To our surprise, a large nutria rat surfaced just three feet from the boat. I opened fire again, as the nutria dove like a submarine being attacked by missiles, only to reappear on the opposite side of the boat. I knew I couldn't be missing, as I took my time and aimed, yet the nutria turned and started toward the boat again. I continued to fire, just as fast as I could reload, and it finally stopped swimming toward us.

There was so much lead in the nutria, I'm surprised it didn't sink to the bottom. It must have weighted twenty five pounds, not counting what I added. With big yellow-orange teeth, it looked really mean and smelled disgusting like an old wet dog.

Proudly I carried the nutria home to show off. Was I ever surprised when Big Mama said to gut it out, and she'd fix it for supper. No way was I going to eat that nasty thing.

It's smell made the house stink so bad, I couldn't stand to be there and walked to Aunt Gwen's, begging to stay the night with my cousins.

For days the house still smelled like that nutria rat, but I learned a valuable lesson. Never bring home anything I didn't want to eat. I learned that some people do eat them, so it could have just been the way it was prepared. Maybe it was just the rat part of the name that turned my stomach.

Just as I was starting to adjust to living in Sweeny, Big Mama received a letter from the Vernon Parish Sheriff in Leesville, wanting her to contact him. While she thought he wanted to discuss the fire, I worried it was about the jail break. Big Mama and Papaw decided it was time to move again, but this time there would be no forwarding address.

I was thinking we would probably go to Arkansas or maybe Oklahoma, but Papaw surprised me when he announced Washington.

"Washington?" I asked, surprised. "Are we going to see the President?"

"No, Washington State. You're going to like it there. Mountains, rushing streams with crystal clear water and lush green forests," Papaw answered. "My sister lives near Spokane. I think this would be a good time to go see her. It looks like it's about 2,300 miles," He mumbled to himself deep in thought, as he planned the route we would take.

I remembered how all these long trips had turned out before. I couldn't help but wonder what the foster home would be like when they got arrested.

Chapter THIRTY-FIVE

P apaw traded our car in for a green 1950 Chevrolet pickup. Buying the truck was essential, as Big Mama had acquired some furniture since the fire. She didn't want to leave it when we moved, and start all over again.

After telling my friends and family goodbye, we left Sweeny bound for what was sure to be another adventure.

Though we were headed to Washington, Papaw planned a few detours along the way. He said that Fredericksburg, Texas has the best peaches in the world, and it was well worth the drive to go there. "I don't know if they have Choctaw pecans in this part of the country, but I'd like to find someplace to buy a few hundred pounds. My sister always mentions in her letters how much she misses being able to buy good pecans in Washington," Papaw added.

"Pull over and stop the damn truck right now." Big Mama yelled. "I mean it!"

"Honey, what's wrong?" Papaw asked with a surprised look on his face.

"You're driving with your head up your ass again. Now pull over—I'm driving."

I didn't see anything wrong with his driving, but I knew better than to say anything.

Papaw stopped beside the highway and traded places with Big Mama, frowning and shaking his head the whole time. There was no point in arguing, he knew that all too well. The words flew back and forth between them as we crossed the Gillespie County line.

"I think it's pretty chicken shit that you want to buy something for your sister, yet you never get me anything."

"Oh, so that's it! Now the truth comes out. You're jealous!" Papaw yelled back. "Well by God you can just let me out right here. I'm not going to put up with this all the way to Washington."

I sat in the middle, looking straight ahead and wishing they would both just go away.

Big Mama didn't waste any time in stopping and letting Papaw out. I watched her as we pulled back on the highway, but neither one of us said anything. We must have traveled about ten miles when I asked her what we were going to do. It was as if I had broken the trance she was in.

"I guess I better go back and get the sorry bastard," she said bluntly.

Big Mama turned around and went about five miles before we met a Gillespie County Sheriff's car. Looking in the rearview mirror as he passed, she let out a long; "Son-of-a-bitch."

I looked back and saw the deputy whip a U-turn behind us, and turn his overhead lights on.

"I didn't do a damn thing wrong, and he's stopping us," Big Mama complained.

As the deputy walked up to her window, Big Mama tore into him; "I want to know what in the hell you stopped me for!"

"Ma'am please just calm down and I'll tell you what's going on. I've got a man in my car that I picked up walking about five miles back down the highway. He says he's married to you and that you drove off and left him. Now if you don't want him with you, I can take him into town. He insisted that if I stopped you, everything would be fine and you'd let him back in the truck. So it's your choice. Do you want him with you or not?"

Big Mama apologized to the deputy and assured him their fighting would stop.

The deputy went back to his patrol car and brought Papaw up to our truck.

"You folks have a good day," the deputy said, as he smiled and walked away.

Papaw had a sheepish grin on his face when he climbed in on the passenger side. Big Mama was still mad.

A trip that most people could have made in three days, was taking us a week at 45 miles per hour. We didn't have to worry about speeding tickets, but the possibility of getting rear-ended was a real danger.

Experience must have taught Big Mama and Papaw that if they really wanted to make it to Washington, they couldn't drink as much as in past trips. They seemed to only hit the bottle when we stopped at rest areas for the night, though we did stop awful early. Big Mama would cook along the way, or sometimes just stop and make coffee. We would usually find another road side park before dark, and sleep there.

As we drove through Idaho, I was overwhelmed with how beautiful the scenery was. I had seen the mountains in New Mexico and Arizona, but here they touched the clouds. No where had I seen such magnificent rivers and thick evergreen forests.

After we passed through Spokane, Papaw drove about 15 miles northwest of the city to an area named Green Bluff. Papaw's sister Beatrice (or Aunt Bea, as I was told to call her) lived with her husband Uncle Howard. I'm sure Aunt Bea was glad to see Papaw, as she hadn't seen him in years, but it was easy to see she wasn't impressed that we intended to move in with them.

Aunt Bea and Uncle Howard's farm was positioned on a ridge, with incredible views of Green Bluff. The area was covered with small bountiful farms and orchards that overlook splendid valleys below.

To the northeast, majestic Mount Spokane stood in all its glory, like a special gift from God. Clouds of mist blowing off its snow capped peak would stall and hang on the ridges before slowly moving down into the valleys. I stood there in awe, knowing I could never get enough of that view. I was going to climb the mountain at the first opportunity.

Fortunately for everyone, there was a small guest cabin, about fifty feet behind Aunt Bea's house that Big Mama and Papaw would stay in, while I was told I could stay in the main house. Aunt Bea was very nice, but I could still feel tension in the air. Uncle Howard seemed nervous and I could tell from the start he wanted to say something.

Before we started unpacking, Uncle Howard walked up to Big Mama and Papaw and made an announcement. "You're welcome to stay here temporarily, but only if you agree to a few rules."

Big Mama and Papaw stood there dumfounded as he continued; "There will be no drinking on this property, nor do I want you around here when you have been drinking. I don't want you smoking in the cabin or in my house. If you can abide by those rules and are willing to look for your own place to live as soon as possible, then we'll get along just fine."

I was impressed. I had never seen anyone tell Big Mama and Papaw how it was going to be, much less without getting an ear full in return. What surprised me most was they agreed to his rules. *Big Mama and Papaw's reputation was known all the way to Washington,* I thought to myself. Maybe Aunt Bea wasn't as distant as I had thought.

In keeping with the tradition of earning my room and board, I helped Uncle Howard around the farm as much as possible. He worked at the Kaiser Aluminum Smelter in Mead, but would line me up with jobs he wanted done each day. Working unsupervised, I fed his cattle, picked up around his pruned apple and cherry trees or moved rocks from the disked ground in his orchard.

In spite of Uncle Howard's rules, Big Mama and Papaw continued to drink, but they tried hard to hide it. I hoped Uncle Howard wouldn't notice, as I liked living there, but their drinking became very evident.

I was helping Uncle Howard work on his tractor, when he

brought it up; "Cliff, I've suspected for the past week that your grandparents are drinking. Have you noticed anything?"

I bit my lip and delayed answering, trying to buy more time. I could tell the truth and get kicked out of paradise, or lie and remain for a few more days. I looked past Uncle Howard at the snow capped peak of Mount Spokane and started to answer when he cut me off.

"You know Cliff, if it wasn't for you, I'd never let them stay here in the first place. I appreciate all the help you've been, but my nerves just can't stand having them around."

"Papaw said he found a house close to the Green Bluff store, and he's just waiting for the owner to give them an answer if we can rent it. They should know any day now."

"Well, as much as I hate it, if they don't have a place by Monday, I'm going to ask them to leave. If it's okay with you, I'm going to offer to let you stay here until they get back on their feet. Would that be okay?"

"That sounds great to me Uncle Howard," I answered with enthusiasm. I wanted to add—"I would stay here forever if you let me," but I didn't want to be faced with rejection should he say no.

Saturday afternoon, just two days after Uncle Howard told me of the deadline, Papaw pulled into the driveway and announced we had the house on Green Bluff. "I hope you're not disappointed Cliff, but the house only has one bedroom. We'll have to buy a couch for you to sleep on, but it's in the country, so I think you'll like it."

I really wanted to say, I'm going to stay here at Uncle Howard's, but he wasn't there to defend me.

We were moved in within an hour, but instead of sleeping in the living room, I asked if I could have the basement.

"Son, have you looked at the basement?" Papaw asked. It only has a dirt floor and no bathroom."

"He wants his privacy," Big Mama broke in. "I know what it's like to have someone looking down your neck, and watching your every move. If he wants the basement for his room, then by God, let him have it."

It was settled—the basement was mine. The entryway was outside the house and down a flight of stairs, with a doorway at the bottom. Though there was no heat, the temperature never dropped below freezing, though at times I could see my breath. A single 75 watt light bulb hung down from the bare wooden rafters and seemed to create its own fog when it was cold. One wall was lined with shelves of dust covered canned fruit, long abandoned by the previous resident.

Because the basement floor was dirt, I placed a two by three foot strip of carpet beside the bed, so I didn't get my feet dirty dressing each morning.

Aunt Bea was very active in the "Green Bluff Home Economics Club" and would stop by our house once in awhile to see if Big Mama wanted to go with her. Maybe being her sister-in-law, she felt obligated to invite her to join the group. Big Mama went a few times, but usually made excuses why she couldn't go. There was just no way that Big Mama could fit in. I'm sure she only went because she felt obligated to Aunt Bea.

When we lived in Bridge City, one of the reasons Big Mama wanted to move was because she didn't like all the do-gooders.

Now, here she was thousands of miles away, being invited to join a Home Economics Club. It's funny how life deals out the cards. I wondered what would happened, if she ever showed up at one of their meetings falling down drunk. Big Mama would probably cuss out anyone she even remotely disliked, and then we'd be moving again.

❦

I had done so well helping Uncle Howard around his farm that Big Mama suggested I may find a job on Green Bluff and help with the family expenses.

"Maybe Uncle Howard would hire me," I suggested.

"That cheap bastard didn't pay you before. You can do better than that," Big Mama criticized. "I saw a help wanted sign tacked on the bulletin board at the Green Bluff store this afternoon. It had the directions and phone number if you want Papaw to take you there."

I agreed and was hired just a few hours later. My new employer was Melvin Walker, a local farmer who lived just a few miles from our house. He raised vegetables that his family sold from a produce stand on the farm. They also had an orchard with apples and cherries. Melvin and his wife Bonny had three children who all worked on the farm. I was treated as an equal, not just a farm hand. It was like I was part of their family. We all worked hard, but it was very rewarding to me. Not so much in monetary value, but just being part of a normal family. The only bad thing was I still had to go home each night.

The Walkers knew that things weren't normal at my house. I could see the suspicion on their faces when Big Mama or Papaw would show up drunk to pick me up after work. On my paydays Big Mama would come to pick up my check even before the Walkers had it made out.

I was never able to keep any of the money I earned and that seemed wrong to me. If I asked questions about what my money was being used for, Big Mama would get angry. Going to the movies or saving enough to buy a motorcycle or car occupied my thoughts. I knew with Big Mama overseeing my money that would never happen.

Big Mama and Papaw didn't like to drive after dark, so if I was late getting off work, Mr. Walker and his wife would drive me home.

On one drive home Mr. Walker asked, "Cliff, how much do your grandparents keep out of each of your checks?"

"It just depends on what bills we have at the time," I answered trying to be evasive out of embarrassment.

"So what is the average amount you get to keep?" Mrs. Walker added.

They were touching on a subject I didn't want to talk about, but it was obvious they weren't going to drop it.

"I don't know, maybe $50.00 or sometimes $25.00," I lied.

"And sometimes nothing?" Mrs. Walker asked, looking back over her shoulder at me inquisitively.

"Yes Ma'am, sometimes," I reluctantly answered. I didn't tell them that my Mom was writing and asking for money. I tried to send her a little each month.

"You know what we ought to do?" Mrs. Walker asked, turning toward her husband. Before he could answer, she continued; "We should just pay Cliff half of what we've been paying him, and then put the other half in a savings account for him. That way, he'll have a nest egg to start life with when he's older. What do you think, Cliff?"

"I don't know," I replied, uncomfortable with the conversation. I was glad that we were almost to my house.

"Well if you decide you want us to do that, we'll be glad to give you a ride to the bank and help you open an account. I just know your grandparents are drinking up all your hard earned money, and it's a crying shame."

Mr. Walker pulled into my driveway. I said goodnight and jumped out before they could ask any more questions. I was glad Mrs. Walker didn't notice my tears. I just couldn't open up and tell them how I really felt. Maybe I just had too much pride to open my heart to anyone. I just couldn't take a chance.

My next paycheck was reduced, and I suspected the Walkers were secretly holding back money for me. This was really thoughtful and considerate, but Big Mama was keeping track of my hours, and raised holy hell. She demanded I quit and find another job. I was upset because if the truth were known; I would have worked for the Walkers for free just to be a part of their family.

Between my paychecks and Papaw's Navy retirement checks, they had been able to stay drunk all month. Now with only Papaw's income, things were a little tougher. When you grow accustomed to an income and then all at once it stops, it puts a strain on your lifestyle. Maybe I should say *their* lifestyle.

The local grocery store cut off their credit the first time they didn't pay their monthly bill. The utility company turned off our power when they were a few months behind. I'm not sure how they pulled it off, but the power was turned back on in my name. Big Mama developed a really bad case of the shakes and would have sold her soul for another bottle.

I felt a twinge of sadness when the summer disappeared, but autumn brought happiness to Green Bluff. The harvest was in full swing as the farmers rushed to get the last crops packed away. Green Bluff had turned to yellows and browns, and snow was again visible above the timber line on Mount Spokane. The promise I had made myself to climb the mountain was still unfulfilled, and now it was time to start yet another new school.

So far I had attended schools in Bridge City, Deweyville, Pasadena, Sweeny, Evans, Cove, Seminole, Burlington and some of them more than once. Mead Jr. High would be the ninth school. I was so far behind scholastically that Big Mama suggested I may want to just drop out. Maybe find a good job packing apples in one of the many packing sheds.

I knew Big Mama's real interest was the money, and I became even more determined to go to school. Thoughts of my future began to unfold. Really important things like girls.

For some strange reason I was instantly one of the most popular kids in school. I didn't understand it, but it was a pleasant change. Maybe it was my strong southern drawl or maybe it had something to do with my manners. If a teacher asked me something I would answer; "Yes sir or yes ma'am." One of the teachers asked me; "Were your parents in the military?"

"Retired military," I answered.

"I can tell," the teacher replied. The other kids in the class laughed, so the teacher went on to talk about respect. I don't think it was just my military connection to Papaw, because most of the kids in the schools I had been to in the south said; "Yes ma'am or no ma'am." It was expected down south and answering; "Yea" may have caused more than just a raised eyebrow.

Chapter THIRTY-SIX

On the first of October the mail lady brought another Navy check to our box. I already knew what condition Big Mama and Papaw would be in even before I arrived home from school.

True to past experiences, I came home to find the house trashed. The smell of burnt beans filled the air. I rushed to the stove and added some water to an almost dry pot. Broken glass covered the linoleum on the kitchen floor. When Big Mama was drinking, housekeeping and cooking weren't on her list of priorities. She was sloppy drunk and still throwing things at Papaw. It looked like every dish in the kitchen had been thrown and pieces was scattered and broken throughout the house.

I sat down on the couch and tried to watch *Bonanza* on television and ignore their fighting. It was hard to concentrate with all the distractions. My thoughts drifted away from the television and the fighting going on around me. I wondered who my dad was and where he lived. Maybe I had brothers or even sisters. I wondered where Rocky was, and if things were any better for him. What would life be like, not living on the wrong side of the river? If it wasn't raining outside, I would have just gone walking in the woods, but it was too nasty for that. To escape the chaos, I turned up the volume on the television, trying to block out what was going on around me.

I couldn't help but wonder what the fight was about this time. Papaw apparently didn't know himself because I heard him ask; "What the hell did I do, babe?"

"Not a damn thing," she answered with a look of repulsion written on her face.

He knew as well as I did, that quarrelling with her was a waste of time. She was impossible to talk to when she was drunk.

"I'm going to go lay down. I'm tired of all this bull shit," Papaw cussed as he stormed off toward the bedroom.

An ashtray flew from Big Mama's hand and crashed into the bedroom door just as Papaw slammed it shut, stringing a trail of cigarette butts and ashes across the floor. She staggered her way back into the kitchen and sat down at the table, dragging the checkered vinyl tablecloth to one side.

Peace at last, I thought to myself as I moved back to the couch. I changed channels and decided on *American Bandstand*. Dick Clark introduced Chubby Checker and he cut loose on *Let's Twist Again*. Not my kind of music, but the cute girls caught my attention.

I had just sat back down on the couch and relaxed with my attention focused on the television when Big Mama entered the room. With bare feet, she tracked through the mess on the linoleum floor then opened the bedroom door. It slammed back against the wall with a bang, the doorknob knocking a hole in the sheetrock. All I could see was her back as she screamed and yelled profanities at Papaw. When he ignored her, she staggered back into the living room and flopped down on the other end of the couch.

Big Mama's head bobbed back and forth like she was fighting to stay awake. I really hoped she would just pass out. The reflection of the television screen bounced back off her glazed over eyes, like what she was watching, never quite made it to her brain. A half smoked cigarette burned slowly into the finish of the end table next to her. I started to bring it to her attention, but stopped. After all it was her table, why should I care? It serves her right.

Big Mama leaned forward and I thought for sure she was going to fall on the floor. Instead, she slid open the drawer on the end table and began rummaging. I grew curious as to what she was looking for as her cigarettes were beside her on the couch, and her bottle was in the kitchen. I was sure that Papaw had the truck keys in his pocket.

To my surprise, she took a box of .22 shells out of the drawer and dumped them on the end table, spilling half of them on the floor. Now she had my full interest! Wheezing heavily, she broke out in a coughing fit and brought both hands to her crotch. She started to say something, but started coughing again. I looked away when I noticed the wet pee stain growing on the couch.

Her body swayed as she struggled to her feet and reached up, taking my .22 rifle from its rack on the wall. With the gun's barrel against the floor, Big Mama used it as a crutch as she tried to load a shell in the chamber. Her coordination was just too impaired to place the bullet in the barrel of the gun.

"Goddamn it," she cursed as she walked toward me with the

.22 shell in one hand and the gun in the other. In her sweetest voice, she asked without emotion; "Cliff, honey, will you load this for me?"

"Sure," I replied, and quickly placed the shell in the chamber. I didn't really think she was capable of taking things to this extreme. It had to be just a bluff, but I decided to play her game. Possibly she was just checking my loyalty to see whose side I was on. Maybe she expected me to talk her out of whatever she had planned.

Calling her bluff, I cocked the rifle and pushed the safety into place (just in case) before handing the gun back to her.

Her facial expression didn't change like I expected. She didn't seem at all surprised that I would help her without knowing what she was going to do.

"Thank you honey," she said sweetly.

"Are you going hunting, Big Mama?"

"You goddamn right I am!" She answered without offering an explanation.

Big Mama staggered back into the kitchen with the rifle.

Curiosity got the best of me. I had to see what she was going to do with the gun.

Peeking around the corner, I could see Big Mama leaning up against the kitchen cupboard with a bottle of whiskey in her hand. Her head was tilted back, and I could hear the whiskey gurgle as it flowed down her throat. The rifle was leaned up against the refrigerator door. Maybe she'll just forget about it, and I can hide the rifle when she's not looking, I reasoned.

She placed the bottle back in the cupboard. As she picked

up the rifle; I ducked back into the living room. I could hear her coming and pretended I was watching television. Just to be on the safe side, I kept a watch out of the corner of my eye. She passed through the living room without saying anything, and into the bedroom where Papaw was snoring. I got off the couch and tiptoed to the doorway to see what she was going to do.

Cautiously, I peeked around the corner of the bedroom doorway. Big Mama was creeping up to the bed with the gun pointed toward Papaw. He was laying face down and had no idea she was even in the room.

I didn't know if I should try to take the rifle away from her, yell out a warning to Papaw, or just pray that she didn't know how to take the rifle off safety.

Big Mama placed the gun barrel against the back of Papaw's head, but he didn't even wake up.

"I'm going to kill you, you worthless bastard," she announced.

"Go ahead," he mumbled in a sarcastic drunken slur. He never even rolled over to see what she was doing.

"I mean it. You're a dead son-of-a-bitch!"

It still didn't seem to faze him. I saw Big Mama flinch as she attempted to pull the trigger, as if expecting to hear a bang, but the rifle wouldn't fire. Fortunately, she didn't think about the rifle's safety. Furious it wouldn't shoot, she grabbed the barrel and brought the stock down hard across the back of his head. His head cracked with a dull thud that reverberated through the room and made me cringe.

I thought he would have been knocked out cold or maybe

she hit him hard enough to kill him, but Papaw jumped up and grabbed the rifle away from her.

Big Mama knew she was in deep trouble and ran for the door to get away from him. I jumped back out of the way as she ran by. Papaw was right behind her, and as they charged through the living room. Blood was thick in Papaw's hair and running down his back. His tee-shirt was stained a dark red, but his injury didn't seem to slow him down.

Big Mama ran outside struggling to keep her balance, looking back over her shoulder as she half ran, half staggered away. Papaw stopped chasing her when he reached the back porch but Big Mama kept going toward the barn.

I hid the rifle behind the couch before Papaw came back inside. He didn't say anything, but went into the bathroom and closed the door. I asked him if he wanted me to check his head but he just said; "Just leave me the hell alone."

Shrugging my shoulders, I went back to see what else was on television. It's really hard to stay involved in a movie or book without losing your place when you have interruptions and distractions like that.

Papaw had been in the bathroom about half an hour when Big Mama came back in looking for him. After checking the bedroom, she asked me where he was.

"I'm not sure," I lied, not wanting her to find him.

I was hoping she would have just passed out in the barn, but we couldn't be that lucky. I could still see the devil in her eyes and knew it wasn't over yet. Poor guy, I thought to myself. Why does he put up with this?

There weren't too many places he could hide in our little

house. When Big Mama opened the bathroom door I almost laughed. There lay Papaw sound asleep in the dry bathtub snoring. Big Mama didn't think it looked funny at all and reached down turning the shower on full force.

He wasn't real quick to wake up, but soon came chasing her again as the steam from the hot water filled the air and drifted out of the bathroom door. This time she made a beeline for the front door and out toward the road in front of the house. Papaw was wet and barefoot, and his head was still dripping blood, so he didn't chase her far before giving up.

Papaw came back inside and out the back door to one of the few places he could go for some peace and quiet—my room in the basement.

It wasn't long before she was back and searching the house for him again.

"Where did the son-of-a-bitch go?" she asked with hate in her blood red eyes?

"I think he went out to the barn or maybe for a walk in the woods," I answered, hoping she would just give up and go to sleep.

When Big Mama went out the backdoor, I peeked out the kitchen window, watching her search behind the house. I hoped she would bypass the basement stairs, and go on to the barn. Instead she turned and started down the stairs toward my room. When she was out of sight, I stepped outside and watched her carefully working her way down the stairs.

After reaching the bottom, she picked up a gallon can of paint that had been stored on the side of the steps. Drawing her arm back, I saw her throw the can into my room. I couldn't see

Papaw from where I was watching, but boy could I hear him.

The paint had barely left Big Mama's hand when she started running up the stairs toward me. She hadn't even made it halfway when Papaw grabbed her by the ankle and dragged her back to the bottom.

I had seen enough. It was time for me to go back to the television. I could still hear her screams coming through the floor below me. I wished I were somewhere else—anywhere but here would be fine.

The rain had turned to a light drizzle but I needed to untangle my mind. I walked across the alfalfa field and down the north slope of Green Bluff into the forest. For hours I wandered aimlessly until my cold wet clothes forced me to return home.

It was well after dark when I climbed the last few feet to the level surface of Green Bluff. The drizzle had turned to a cold rain. My mind wanted me to believe that what I had experienced was all a bad dream, but I knew better. I really expected someone to be dead, just laying there at home waiting for me to find the body.

Walking back across the field, I could see there were no lights on in our house. The fact the house was still there was a good sign. At least Big Mama hadn't burned this one down. I wondered what, if anything I would find in my room. That's where I last heard Big Mama screaming.

Quietly, I walked down the dark stairs to my room. Thank God, no one was there; dead or alive. The room had the combined stench of beer and mold. I noticed in the dim light a half empty beer bottle laying on its side on the floor, its spilled contents had turned the dirt floor a darker color. Red paint was splattered on the cement wall above the bed. The empty gallon paint can was on my pillow with wet, red paint still soaking into the pillow and bedding.

I stripped the bedding, but even the mattress was wet with paint. There was no movement upstairs. I couldn't help but wonder what had happened after I left. Laying on the edge of the bare mattress to avoid the wet paint, I drifted in and out of sleep.

Dreams throughout the night would jar me awake. I just couldn't get the image of Big Mama holding the rifle to Papaw's head out of my mind. In one dream, Big Mama told everyone that I had murdered Papaw with my rifle. Teams of law enforcement were searching the mountains looking for me.

Thankfully, the sound of someone walking around upstairs woke me. Without windows in my room it was hard to tell if it was morning yet. Pulling the string attached to the light above my bed, I squinted in the bright light. It was only 5:30 AM. My alarm wouldn't ring for another half an hour.

Cold, I lay back down and listened to the footsteps, trying to decide who they belonged to. Soon I could hear a second set of footsteps in the kitchen that sounded like Papaw's. Relieved they had both survived the night; I dressed for school and went upstairs.

Big Mama was hobbling around on one leg complaining of pain in her ankle, while she tried to sweep up the broken glass and cigarette butts that covered the floor. Papaw was in the bathroom shaving his head. His hair was thick with dried red paint and coagulated blood. No one said anything about the night's events. The mood was eerily silent. I fixed myself some toast and blackberry jelly and went out early to wait for the school bus.

For the next week if anyone asked Big Mama what happened to her ankle, she would say that she slipped on the ice and fell. I don't know what excuse Papaw used for his injuries but they always seemed to protect each other.

Chapter THIRTY-SEVEN

I learned to drive over the summer, and took advantage of my new skills anytime Big Mama and Papaw were drinking and wanted to go somewhere. Though I wasn't old enough for a driver's license, I'm sure they realized I could get them safely to where they wanted to go. Big Mama convinced Papaw that even if I were stopped by the police, the fine for not having a driver's license would be much less than for drunk driving, so I became their chauffeur.

On Sunday morning while most of the families on Green Bluff were headed to church, Big Mama and Papaw would be arguing about which bar they were going to. Every Sunday was the same old routine.

Papaw preferred the bars across the Idaho state line near Post Falls, but traffic was always heavy there and that bothered Big Mama. A little greater distance, the small town of Blanchard, Idaho was on the opposite side of Mount Spokane and we could drive back roads to get there.

I preferred Blanchard, as the bar was more kid friendly, and it took longer to get there. If a band was playing, I'd watch their every move and daydream of owning a guitar. Big Mama would talk the band into letting me sing a song once or twice during the afternoon. The drunker the crowd became, the more they enjoyed my singing. Big Mama would pass the hat and usually collect two or three dollars, then give me the money to play pool or pinball games.

One Sunday we had been at the bar most of the afternoon when Big Mama got into an argument with some of the other customers. When the bartender told her she was cut off, he received the normal tongue lashing I knew was forth coming. Papaw pulled her to the door as she told most of the people present what she thought of them.

As I drove away, she started cussing Papaw for not sticking up for her. "After all," as she put it; "You're supposed to be a man, but I've yet to see anything resembling that."

Big Mama was sitting in the middle of our pickup as I drove the back roads towards Green Bluff. Her cigarette smoke was irritating my eyes so I asked Papaw if he could crack his window and let in some fresh air.

"You've got a window. Why don't you roll yours down?" Big Mama glared toward me, waiting for an answer.

"If I do it just draws all your cigarette smoke to my side of the truck."

She shot another sarcastic snarl in my direction; "You're driving too damn fast, now slow down."

I looked at the speedometer and was doing almost fifty. There was no point in arguing, so I slowed down to forty. "That's better," she replied, with a look on her face like she had won some great victory. I was back under her control, so she started on poor Papaw again. She had been cussing him constantly for about five miles. I didn't understand what he did wrong and I'm not sure he did himself, but it didn't matter. She didn't need a reason. His ignoring her seemed to irritate her even more.

All at once Big Mama's whole mood changed. She became really nice and apologized for acting like she did. She put her arm over Papaw's shoulders and snuggled up close to him. I couldn't believe the change, and watched in amazement as she turned to kiss him on the cheek. She had never apologized before, or even tried to make up when they fought. This had to be a first. Papaw seemed surprised himself.

"Don't worry about it, baby," he replied as he patted her on the leg and returned a kiss. "If that damn bar doesn't want our business, we'll just find one you like."

Big Mama snuggled up to Papaw and gave him a big hug. As Papaw kissed her again, Big Mama reached across Papaw's lap and opened the door with her left hand. She tried desperately to push him out of the pickup.

I stomped on the brakes and was almost to a stop before Papaw realized what she was trying to do. His face had a look of disbelief. She was still trying to shove him out the door with both hands, even though we were stopped. Convinced it wasn't just his imagination, he turned and hit her in the face with his fist.

Blood was dripping from Big Mama's nose as Papaw jumped out and started walking away from the truck. Her eyes flashed with fire as she turned to me.

"Are you going to let him get away with that?"

"I think you deserved what you got," I answered without thinking of the consequences.

"What did you say?" She arched one eyebrow.

Before I could repeat myself, she slapped me across my face so hard it popped. Big Mama half fell, half jumped out of the pickup and slammed the door as hard as she could. I jumped as the window fell off its track inside the door. She started walking in the opposite direction of Papaw, back toward the Idaho state line.

It was hard to fight back the burning in my eyes, but I was too angry to cry. Looking in the rearview mirror, Big Mama was still walking, and Papaw hadn't looked back.

I was tired of the bullshit; tired of living like a misfit outside the normal world that surrounded me. It was time I started making my own decisions. I drove past Papaw without even looking at him. I had learned by necessity to roll with the punches, but no more. I was sick of this lifestyle and wanted out.

It was almost dark when I pulled into our driveway. I hung the truck keys on the nail in the kitchen and checked the refrigerator for something to eat. Not much to pick from. Nothing but a block of cheese in a brown cardboard box printed with the words U.S. Government. After cutting myself three thick slices, I retreated to my room hoping Big Mama and Papaw wouldn't kill me when they found a way home.

My alarm went off at 6:30 a.m... I listened for footsteps above me, but there was nothing but silence. Surely they must have found a ride home, unless they were in jail.

I went upstairs and discovered Big Mama and Papaw were still sleeping. Quietly, I cut myself two more slices of cheese and gently closed the refrigerator door.

Waiting for the school bus, I hoped they wouldn't wake up until after I was gone. I worried all day about what my punishment would be when I came home.

When I came home from school, it was as if nothing had happened. I became a part in the silent code they shared. Anything that was done or had been said was never talked about again. Neither of them even seemed angry.

All week I thought about Sunday and Big Mama slapping me. Even though we didn't talk about it, I wouldn't forget. Maybe it's my Cajun blood—If someone makes me mad, I stay that way for a long time. Another Sunday afternoon drinking trip to Idaho would be coming in a few days, but I wasn't going; I had a mountain to climb.

CHAPTER
THIRTY-EIGHT

I knew Big Mama and Papaw would never agree to let me climb Mount Spokane, so I mentioned wanting to explore some beaver ponds below Uncle Howard's place. I talked Papaw into dropping me off early Sunday morning. I figured I could get Uncle Howard to give me a ride home later in the day.

Uncle Howard had warned me that climbing the mountain in the winter would be crazy. He said the winter conditions at that elevation would be extreme, not to mention the possibility of avalanches and getting lost. His advice just added to the excitement of such an adventure, and meant I wouldn't be able to tell anyone.

A light rain was falling, but his trip had been planned far too long to cancel. I fixed myself three potted meat sandwiches, cut four large slices of cheese and wrapped them in a plastic bag to keep everything dry.

Papaw saw Uncle Howard was home and didn't want to stop, so I had him drop me off a little further down the road. *"Great, it's just that much closer to the mountain,"* I thought.

Papaw wasn't even out of sight before the cold rain made me reconsider the idea of climbing the mountain. With nothing else to do, I decided not to turn back.

I followed the road up the back side of the 5,883 feet peak, but I soon found it was blocked by snow and there was more falling. At first there was only a few inches, but the higher I went, the deeper the snow became.

By the time I reached a small saddle between two peaks, the snow was above my knees. Wet and freezing cold, I again considered turning back. The wind was blowing waves of snow which made it hard to see, but I kept going.

A small sign coated with ice, pointed out Mt. Kit Carson to the right. To my left, hidden somewhere in the dark rolling clouds was Mount Spokane. I could see the peak of Mount Kit Carson was just a short distance away and decided to climb that mountain instead.

Other than the deep snow, the climb was easier than I had thought. After reaching the top, I sat down on a large wind blown granite outcrop for lunch. At times, breaks in the storm would offer views of the valley and Green Bluff far below.

When I turned to leave, I was surprised to see Mount Spokane in all its glory beaming in the sunlight that filtered in between the dark storm clouds. It's said the mountain derives its name from an Indian word which means "sun." The mountain was spectacular, a real spiritual experience in itself. I knew I couldn't turn back now, I had to keep climbing.

Another dark cloud enveloped the mountain, but I had seen the top and there was no turning back. The storm again blocked out the sun, and the snow made it hard to see where I was going. I was totally disoriented, but only one direction mattered, and that was up. Maybe it was hardhead-ness, but something forced me to keep going.

Stopping to rest before leaving the timber line, I enjoyed a few deep breaths of the fresh smell of spruce, and ponderosa pine blowing in the north wind. Old growth timber was coated on one side with snow, and the other with moss or lichen. The area was completely void of any signs of wildlife. Combined with the odor of decaying timber and the eerie silence on the mountain, I decided it was time to keep moving.

I was cutting a fresh trail waist deep as I hiked up from the timber line, slowly making my way toward the top of the mountain.

After reaching the summit, the view was the most beautiful sight I had ever witnessed in my life. Between the snow squalls, the sun would break through between the clouds and shine off the distant snow covered trees. Ice crystals made miniature rainbows and cast their colors in the air.

Every direction I looked was the most beautiful winter wonderland you could imagine. I just stood there in the center of the universe, soaking it all in. In the far valleys I could see rivers and beautiful dark blue lakes. The sight was incredible. The air was so fresh I had to catch my breath and hold it in.

No one in their right mind could see this and think for one minute that there isn't a God. Though I was wet and cold, I could feel "His" presence around me. Snow covered everything, yet unexplainable warmth radiated from the mountain. A sense of significance far beyond my comprehension flowed through me.

A realization came that if I wanted to change my life, it would be up to me to do so. No one would do it for me. Change was in the air, and it wasn't just the storm blowing in around me.

I had been there for almost an hour, talking to God and thinking about my future, when a dark cloud engulfed the mountain. It was snowing and blowing so hard I couldn't see ten feet in front of me. Fear overrode my spiritual experience and told me it was time to go while I still could. Mount Spokane is known to receive upwards of 300 inches of snow, and I could see myself becoming lost and buried in snow too deep to even move.

Playing it safe, I decided I better follow my tracks back down the mountain so I didn't get lost in the storm. The snow was already covering my tracks, as I plowed back down the mountain side.

About hundred feet above the timberline, I had a surprise that stopped me cold. Huge tracks leading away from mine, continued on around the side of the mountain. Something with huge feet had followed me from the timberline part way up the mountain. I studied the tracks just long enough to see that whatever made the imprints had been walking on its hind feet. The tracks were so fresh, the snow hadn't even started to cover them.

I started to panic. It's the middle of winter—shouldn't bears be hibernating? Why was it following me up the mountain? I had seen enough and took off running down the mountain.

After reaching the timber, I discovered where its tracks had come across mine. It looked like it had been walking on its hind feet the whole time, staying just below the timberline until it came across my tracks, and then followed me. Perhaps it had seen me coming back down the mountain and had run back into the forest to hide. I continued to run for miles, wondering what had made the tracks.

It wasn't until I reached the road leading to Green Bluff that I started feeling safe again. I was almost back to Uncle Howard's when someone stopped and offered me a ride as far as the Green Bluff Store.

By the time I walked on home, it was dark. Big Mama and Papaw were already there and I could hear them fighting as I walked up the driveway. As much as I wanted to tell them about Mount Spokane and my experiences on the mountain, I couldn't. For one thing, they probably wouldn't believe me and if by chance they did, I would be in trouble for going there.

It was only after going to school and telling my friends, that I heard stories about the legendary Big Foot or Sasquatch. I kicked myself the rest of the week for succumbing to my fears and not following the tracks to see what made them.

CHAPTER

THIRTY-NINE

The colder the temperature registered on the Nesbitt's Orange Soda thermometer nailed to the back porch, the more frequent Big Mama and Papaw talked about moving south.

"Even the damn birds fly south for the winter, but we're too stupid to move. We just sit here and freeze our asses off," Big Mama complained.

Over the month of December their conversations changed from if we move, to when and where we were going. Papaw said we would like Broken Bow, Oklahoma or maybe go even further south around Idabel, Oklahoma.

I liked Washington and didn't want to go anywhere. Though my home life and living conditions left a lot to be desired, I had many reasons to want to stay. I was popular in school, had a lot of friends and my grades were improving. Add to that the mountains, trees, and streams. Washington offered everything that I felt was important.

January arrived with an Arctic blast of cold air that seemed to settle in my room. I woke up freezing and unable to control my chattering teeth. Forcing my stiff body out of bed, I could feel the cold coming up through the rug on the dirt floor. I made a dash up the stairs and glanced at the thermometer as I ran in the back door. It read five degrees below zero. Big Mama and

Papaw stood with their backs to the open oven door trying to stay warm.

"See why we want out of this damn place? I can't even make coffee or flush the toilet because the damn water's frozen." I could see her breath as she cussed.

I had rejected the idea of moving and was even trying to figure out a way I could stay, but the cold temperature had brought me around to their way of thinking.

"When are we leaving?" I asked, hoping they would say right now.

"Just as soon as Papaw gets his next check. I'm going to start packing today. You may as well tell the principal that you won't be back to school after Friday. They can transfer your records when we find out where we're going to be."

For the next week I studied the map, following the line Papaw had marked in blue ink; from Washington across the tip of Idaho to Butte, Montana, then south down through Idaho Falls to Salt Lake City. From there his line led on down through the corner of Colorado, across New Mexico, Texas, and on to Broken Bow, Oklahoma.

"Since we're going through Colorado anyway, couldn't we go through Burlington?" I asked. "The last birthday card I got from Aunt Verna and Uncle Mel said they had moved back there. Rocky is living in Burlington, too, and I'd really like to see him again."

"This ain't gonna be no damn vacation," Big Mama reminded me. "We're going to take the most direct route and that's sure as hell not through Burlington."

I studied the map again and added up the miles. It looked to me as if they were purposely avoiding Burlington. The more I thought about Uncle Mel and Aunt Verna, the more I missed them. After all, who had taken me all the way from Colorado to Texas when I had planned to run away? And there was the time when Uncle Mel had driven all the way to Texarkana, and rescued me from the foster home. He gave me a place to live when no one else would. It was obvious they must care about me.

The change I felt in the air on Mount Spokane, was building into a full blown whirlwind in my mind. I found Big Mama and Papaw's lifestyle repulsive and knew I could do better. I wanted out, but just didn't know how to make it happen. One thing was sure; I intended to find out.

As I studied the map, I considered the possibilities. I could just tell Big Mama and Papaw I didn't want to continue living with them, but I knew how that would go over. It would be easier to just walk away at some point. It's a chicken way out I admit, but better than a direct confrontation and getting hit.

The nearest Papaw's route came to Burlington was Green River, Utah. That is if we even made it that far before they were arrested, or had an accident. Adding up the distances between Green River and Burlington, I came up with just over 500 miles. Like some strange omen, 500 Miles by Peter, Paul and Mary began playing on the radio. *"And I'm just 500 miles away from home."* Could a fourteen year old boy hitchhike 500 miles without getting picked up by the police? Maybe, look how far I made it when I was 9 years old, back in Arkansas. I guess I would soon find out.

✤

The day before Papaw's check arrived, he built a wooden frame in the back of his truck and planned to cover it with a tarp, making a makeshift camper shell.

I was somewhat surprised when Papaw enlisted my help in stealing the tarp that covered the neighbor's lumber pile. He noticed my shocked look and explained that we needed it worse than the neighbor did.

Papaw reminded me that we wouldn't be sleeping in motels. "Would you rather sleep out in the snow and rain?" He asked. It was already freezing cold, and a lot of the trip would be through the mountains, so maybe the tarp wasn't such a bad idea.

That night after the neighbor's lights went out we crawled in from the trees behind their house and quietly slipped the tarp off their lumber pile. Their dog barked a little, but that was nothing new. It barked all the time anyway.

As we carried the tarp back towards the house it dawned on me that this is where he got the wood for the frame, too.

Early the next morning we loaded the pickup. Papaw cut the tarp to fit the frame and tied it down with clothesline rope. We were on the road before daylight and crossed into Idaho as the sun's orange glow illuminated the mountain tops. I hated to leave this area, but I promised myself someday I would return. We were headed toward Oklahoma on a highway paved with uncertainty.

Papaw stopped at a liquor store when we reached Idaho. By the time we arrived in Missoula, Montana, they were both too intoxicated to drive. To my relief, Papaw turned the driving over to me. Before I even pulled back on the highway, Big Mama warned me about my speed.

When I reached Deer Lodge, Montana, they had me stop at a store for another bottle of whiskey and a bathroom break. As we climbed back into the truck, Papaw crawled into the back so he wouldn't have to listen to Big Mama and her bitching. At times I felt like doing the same thing, but if she drove the results could be disastrous.

I enjoyed driving more when they were both passed out because I could cover a lot more miles faster. I would keep one eye on the road and the other on Big Mama, and cruise along at a comfortable sixty to seventy miles per hour. God forbid if she woke up.

We were approaching the turnoff just before Butte, Montana when I had an idea. Big Mama and Papaw were both passed out and would probably stay that way most of the day. Why not try and get as close to Burlington as I could before running away? Maybe I could even make it all the way to Burlington without them waking up.

Looking at the map as I drove, I figured I would just continue on to Billings, Montana and then turn south through Wyoming into Colorado. Big Mama and Papaw would be mad if they woke up, but I could just play dumb and act like I didn't know any better.

Big Mama woke up a few times but didn't even have a clue we were off route. She'd just take another long swig from the bottle and lay back down. Papaw was either passed out, or froze to death in the back of the pickup.

A problem I hadn't considered came up when I noticed the fuel gauge read almost empty. The next possible stop was Big Timber, Montana. I would be forced to wake them, since they had the money for the gas. I was getting hungry anyway and needed a bathroom break. Big Timber would be as good a place as any for them to find out I was off their route.

I pulled up to the gas pump at a small country store and woke up Big Mama. Maybe Papaw would just keep sleeping. That would be okay too, as he would be the one to ask where we were.

To my disappointment, Papaw climbed out of the back and headed for the store. He needed more whiskey like General Custer needed more Indians. Big Mama staggered toward the store looking for the restroom. A group of men setting on a bench in front laughed as she swayed past them.

I felt dirty—not just dirty on the outside but on the inside as well. The men watched Papaw as he staggered back toward the truck. The front of his button-fly jeans were left open, showing his white shorts.

As I pumped gas into the truck, one of the men pointed toward me and our pickup with its home-made canvas-covered camper. I could hear them laughing. I gave them the meanest frown I could.

Their attention turned to Big Mama as she swayed out the door using the side of the building for support. Though her vision had to be blurred, she could see that the men were watching her. She stuck her chin in the air and attempted to walk prim and proper, like a high society southern belle in her plaid pants.

"What are you looking at—you sons-a-bitches? Haven't you ever seen a lady before?"

Her audience stared in shock, and then burst out laughing! Big Mama turned their way, giving the group a tidal wave of obscenities. Even in the cold, I could feel the heat of embarrassment creep up my face. I wanted to just drive off and leave them both in Montana. Instead I asked Papaw for the money to pay for the gas and went inside. Some of the men were still laughing as I walked by, but I avoided looking at them. I promised myself that when I was older and married; my kids would never be exposed to the embarrassment I went through.

I continued driving well after dark and made it past the Entering Wyoming sign, silently thanking God that Big Mama and Papaw were asleep. Big Mama was drunk enough I could have told her the sign said Leaving Wyoming and she may not have known the difference.

When I could no longer keep my eyes open, I stopped at a small rest area for the night. Big Mama had sprawled out over most of the seat and there wasn't room in the back with Papaw, so I looked for a place to sleep outside. I could see the rest area was surrounded by sagebrush. Maybe I had read too many old western stories about cowboys waking up with a rattlesnake in their sleeping bag. Just to play it safe, I made myself a bed on top of a cement picnic table.

The cold wind chilled me, and I was anxious for morning's light to come so we could get back on the road and warm up. At the same time, I worried what would happen if Big Mama and Papaw asked where we were.

I woke up to the intense aroma of coffee brewing and rolled over on my hard bed to see Papaw adding dried sagebrush to the campfire beside the picnic table. The warmth of the fire looked inviting, but I dreaded facing Papaw's question of where we were. Big Mama was digging around in a box in the back of the truck. They both looked sober and that could mean doomsday for me. Maybe I could just act like I was sleeping until they were both drunk again. It was a plan, but it wasn't a good plan since I needed to go to the bathroom, and they were drinking coffee, not whiskey. I lay there until I couldn't hold it any longer.

"Good morning," I called, as I ran past Papaw for the bathroom. Big Mama was climbing out of the pickup with three coffee cups in her hands.

I stalled as long as possible in the cinderblock bathroom before joining Big Mama and Papaw by the fire.

"So, where are we?" he asked.

Paralyzed by indecision, I almost choked on my coffee, but it gave me more time to think of an answer.

"I'm not real sure," I lied. "I drove late last night until I couldn't stay awake."

Papaw went to the truck and came back with the map. He had a concerned look on his face as his finger followed the ink line across New Mexico. The wind tore at the map as Papaw followed the line on across the Texas panhandle into Oklahoma.

"Do either of you want more coffee?" Big Mama asked with her hand shaking.

Papaw didn't answer; his full attention was on the map. I shook my head no, as she poured what was left in the pot on the fire.

As Papaw checked the oil on our pickup, I asked if I could drive but was turned down. Papaw noticed we were getting low on gas. "I wonder how far it is to the next town," he grumbled.

We hadn't gone far when I noticed we were approaching a sign. "Look you guys—antelope," I yelled, pointing toward the sage covered hills. Big Mama looked but couldn't see anything. Papaw's attention was focused on the sign, and my attempt to distract him didn't work. He had the answer to his question in bold letters: BUFFALO 14 miles. A puzzled look covered his face as he picked up the map and tried to unfold it with one hand.

"Damn-it, if you're going to read the map, just pull over and let Cliff drive before you kill us," Big Mama snarled.

Papaw pulled off on the shoulder and scanned the New Mexico map, but couldn't find Buffalo. He pulled back on the highway and still had a puzzled look on his face, when ten minutes later, we entered Buffalo. Most of the vehicles in town all had Wyoming license plates, but their attention was focused on the liquor store. After replenishing their supply, we stopped at a gas station and filled the tank.

Papaw counted the money he had left in his billfold and asked Big Mama how much she had. She pulled the whiskey bottle away from her lips just long enough to answer; "What— do you think I'm holding out on you?"

"Damn-it-to-hell, I just asked you a simple question." Papaw reached for the bottle and drank until the bottle was half empty.

I could see the anger building inside Big Mama and fighting

to break loose.

"What in the hell are you trying to prove? Just stop the truck right now. If you're going to drink like a damn fish, then Cliff can drive."

I fought back a smile as Papaw pulled to the side of the road and stopped. I was hoping Papaw would climb in the back again, but instead he got in on the passenger side.

Big Mama took another drink, and I watched as what was left of the bottle drained down. She noticed I was watching her and yelled; "Keep your eyes on the road." And keep it at less than fifty miles per hour, I silently reminded myself.

They were both still arguing when I passed the sign that read Casper 115, Cheyenne 295 miles. Thank God they didn't see the sign, but at the rate they were draining the bottle, I was sure they would want to stop at the next available liquor store.

I had driven about forty miles with Big Mama trying to pick an argument with Papaw the whole time. He tried to explain that he only asked about the money because he was worried if we would have enough to make it to Oklahoma. She ignored his explanation and stared straight ahead as if someone had placed an invisible wall between them.

Though it was cold and windy, I rolled my window part way down in an attempt to draw out the cigarette smoke that filled the cab. I knew better than to ask Papaw to crack his. Big Mama glared at me anyway, and then turned her attention back to Papaw, who was busy counting the money in his billfold.

As fast as a rattlesnake striking, she grabbed the money out of his wallet and thrust her hand in front of my face, throwing the money out the window. I ducked, thinking she was going to hit me, then fought the steering wheel to bring our pickup back in control. It took a few seconds before what had happened registered with Papaw.

"What in the Goddamn hell are you doing?" Papaw drew his hand back with a clinched fist like he was going to hit her, and then stopped in midair. "Cliff, turn around and go back. We have to find the money."

Big Mama had a satisfied look on her face, like she had accomplished some great feat.

I made a U-turn and went back, but it was impossible to tell exactly where we were when she had tossed the money. The wind was blowing full force across the highway, and any paper would be scattered for miles on the open prairie.

Papaw watched the fence-line as I drove slowly along the highway. He let out a yell when he spotted a bill caught in the bunch grass. We searched in vain for hours and were able to recover a few bills caught in the sage brush, but most of it was gone.

I spotted a twenty, still tumbling along the ground and grabbed it when Papaw wasn't looking. Payback I told myself, as I slipped the bill into my pocket. After all, twenty dollars was a small amount, compared to all the money they borrowed from me on Green Bluff. I knew I could kiss the possibility of them ever repaying me goodbye. I may just have to spend it on gas to avoid waking them farther down the road. If I don't have to use it, at least I'll have a little cash to start my new life.

"You do have the keys with you?" Papaw asked.

"Right here in my pocket, why?" I answered.

His outrage came forth in a torrent; "Because the stupid bitch would probably drive off and leave us here if you didn't. I don't know why the hell I put up with her shit."

When we could no longer stand the frigid wind and the possibility of finding additional money was next to none, we walked back toward the highway. It sounds strange, but the pickup looked lonely and out of place; parked in the ditch with the canvas tarp flapping in the wind.

Big Mama had climbed into the back of the truck and was sleeping. One down and one to go, I told myself. I won't have to live this way much longer.

If for some reason Aunt Verna and Uncle Mel turned me down, I was still going to stay in Burlington anyway. The dislike I had in the past for the city was changing. As much as I had detested it in the past, I looked forward to going back. Something inside me had changed.

Papaw was soon fast asleep. For the next hour I avoided bumps on the highway and maintained a steady speed, trying to avoid anything that might wake them.

I held my breath as a Wyoming State Trooper came up behind me and slowed to my fifty five miles per hour, as if he were checking my driving. What could I say if he stopped me? Would I go to jail for not having a driver's license? He followed me for about half a mile, and then raced around to pass. The trooper looked me over, so I waved like I'd been driving all my life. He waved back, then picked up his speed and was soon out of sight.

It was starting to snow, and I was forced to slow down as

we entered Casper. Papaw repositioned himself and belched. I was hoping he would go back to sleep, but he raised his head and looked around.

"Looks like Amarillo. Can you believe this shit? We drive all the way from Washington and don't run into snow until we get to Texas. If you see a liquor store, be sure and stop."

But of course, I told myself. "We better gas up again," I added, fighting back a smile. Boy will he be mad when he finds out we're not in Texas.

Big Mama slept through both the liquor store and fueling stop. I watched her as I filled the tank and saw her arm move so I knew she hadn't frozen to death.

"Maybe we should just stay here tonight, with it snowing like this," Papaw remarked.

"Its okay, the road's not slick and I'd like to just keep going."

"Well if it starts getting bad, you better stop. We don't want to get caught out on the highway in a blizzard."

And we don't want to spend the night here and have you ask where we are in the morning, I chuckled to myself.

"Wow, look at that Papaw!" I pointed toward the passenger window at the vast range-land, taking his attention away from the sign we were approaching: Cheyenne 178 miles. Ha, it worked again! Papaw was still scanning the horizon. I covered my mouth to hide my smile.

"I don't see anything. What the hell was it?" Papaw demanded.

"I don't know. Maybe it was some kind of bird or low flying airplane. I'm surprised you didn't see it," I responded. Papaw looked again, but nothing was there. This was starting to become fun.

Within an hour Papaw was snoring louder than the highway noise. I was almost hypnotized by the endless highway and blowing snow.

My mind was a few hundred miles away in Burlington, when I heard a horn honking behind me. Looking back in the rearview mirror, I could see a car flashing its lights. The driver was waving to get my attention. There was plenty of time to pass, but I moved over to give him more room.

Driving with two wheels on the shoulder was kicking up a lot of snow. He was still flashing his lights and honking. I couldn't understand what the problem was. I glanced back again just in time to see a bottle hit the pavement and break in front of his car. Great, Big Mama must be awake! That explained it all.

I stopped as quickly as I could and pulled off on the shoulder. Fortunately, the other car didn't stop, but laid on his horn as he passed. Papaw woke up and asked what was going on.

"Big Mama is throwing things out the back," I answered matter-of-factly.

"Son-of-a-bitch, I can't close my eyes for a damn minute without her pulling something."

We both went to the back of the pickup in time to see her climb over the tailgate and fall to the gravel. Papaw tried to break her fall but instead landed on top of her. I tried to help both of them back on their feet, but Big Mama pulled away.

She knelt down, dropped her pants and urinated right there in front of the world. Two trucks passing by laid on their air horns as she yelled obscenities and flipped them the finger.

Embarrassed, I walked back to the driver's side of our pickup in disgust, pelted by a torrent of snow the passing trucks kicked up. Laying my head on the steering wheel, I was over come with the feeling of nausea. The whole scene was disgusting beyond words.

Big Mama climbed into the center next to me and lit a cigarette. Her pants were wet and smelled of urine. I cracked the window an inch, chancing Big Mama complaining, but had to have fresh air.

Looking in the side mirror, I could see Papaw with one hand on the truck relieving himself. Passing cars could see him, but he was unconcerned. He tied down the tarp and climbed in on the passenger side next to Big Mama.

"Why in the hell were you throwing things out the back?" Papaw asked.

"Because I couldn't get Cliff to stop," she snapped back. "I tried knocking on the back window. If he didn't have the Goddamn radio cranked all the way up, maybe he'd know what's going on around him."

"I'm sorry, all I could hear was the tarp slapping in the wind," I answered.

We passed another mileage sign, but it was coated with snow so I didn't have to resort to my—"Hey, look over there trick."

Fortunately it wasn't long before their fifth of whiskey was half gone, and they were both sound asleep.

Street lights illuminated our faces, and Big Mama raised her head as we passed through Cheyenne.

"Where are we?"

"Oklahoma City," I lied.

"I think we better stop here for the night."

"There's a snow storm right behind us Big Mama. If I stop we may get stranded here," I explained. "Besides, I'm not even tired and in just a few more hours we should be there."

"Okay, but keep your speed down to forty. This rain will be turning to ice." She pulled her blanket up higher, and leaned over against Papaw.

CHAPTER FORTY

I breathed a sigh of relief and silently thanked God when we passed the *Welcome to Colorful Colorado* sign. I felt a warmth in my chest as the motor hummed along at a steady seventy miles per hour. Big Mama and Papaw were both sound asleep.

The cities of Greeley, Fort Morgan, Brush and Yuma all flew by as images of my life echoed with each passing mile. My sanctuary from the insanity was drawing near.

Entering the city of Wray, I turned south on highway 385 for the last fifty-six mile stretch into Burlington. With a tired smile, I picked up my speed. No matter what happened at this point I would make it. I could walk to Burlington if I had to.

The snow had stopped, allowing the moon to peek out between the dark clouds in the western sky. Crossing the bridge over the South Fork of the Republican River, I glanced off into the darkness and could make out the water shining in the moonlight.

How symbolic, I thought to myself. My whole life has been a river made of memories, and now there was one last bridge to cross. It reminded me of how and why I got here. For years I had lived on the wrong side of the river, but somehow things were going to be different now. A sense of purpose came over me. I had passed to the right side and wouldn't be going back.

The blinking lights of a grain elevator on the southern horizon told me I was approaching Burlington. A trip that had taken fourteen years was about to end.

Pulling up to the curb in front of Uncle Mel's, I was glad to see his car parked in the driveway. I really didn't have a back up plan in case he had moved.

I turned the truck off for what I knew would be my last time, ready for the battle that was bound to come. My moment of truth had arrived.

Nether Big Mama or Papaw awoke as I opened the trucks door and slipped out. They were sure to find out where we were, but I needed time alone with Aunt Verna and Uncle Mel. I needed to ask the hardest question I had ever had the courage to ask anyone: "Can I live with you?"

Aunt Verna and Uncle Mel were shocked to see me. I rushed through the events leading up to my being there, at times almost tripping on the words, and fighting back tears.

I cringed at the sound of pounding on the front door, interrupting the question I was about to ask.

When Uncle Mel opened the door, Big Mama charged in ready to fight. "What in the hell are we doing here?" She yelled.

"I came here because this is where I want to be," I answered timidly.

"You get your ass in the damn truck right now!"

Aunt Verna came to my defense; "He's not going anywhere—he's staying with us."

Big Mama's eyes were still focused on me, like she hadn't even heard what Aunt Verna said. She took a couple of steps toward me, with her fists doubled up, still demanding I leave.

As she drew her arm back to hit me, Aunt Verna grabbed her arm and spun her around. She half pushed/half pulled Big Mama to the front door and told her she wasn't welcome there.

I was surprised she left without a full blown fight, but the pickup hadn't started yet. I had a few things in the truck I would have liked to retrieved, but it wouldn't be worth the hassle.

About fifteen minutes later, another knock on the door told us it wasn't over yet. This time it was Papaw asking if they could camp in the front yard until morning. He promised they would be gone first thing in the morning, and wouldn't cause any problems. Papaw was easy going and good natured. It was easy to want to help him. Uncle Mel was about to say yes, when the phone rang.

The next door neighbor called saying something very disgusting was taking place in the front yard. A very intoxicated older lady had her pants down to her knees, urinating on the lawn!

Aunt Verna's face turned pale, and then changed to red as her blood started to boil. She stormed out of the house and tore into Big Mama with years of repressed rage. Aunt Verna ordered Big Mama and Papaw off the property immediately or she was calling the police.

With no goodbyes, I watched from the front porch as their pickup rattled off down the street and disappeared into the darkness. I wondered what would become of them, and if they could make it to where ever they were going without me.

The sound of a train cut through the darkness, it's mournful whistle resonating off the grain elevators along Railroad Avenue.

The soft clatter of boxcars soon faded into the night west of town. I felt a tinge of sadness that is hard to explain. It took me back to another time long ago. A time when the sound of ships horns would drift across Sabine Lake as they passed under the Rainbow Bridge, announcing their departure for other parts of the world.

Still I felt like I had made the right decision. It was time for a change. I had seen enough of the wrong side of the river. Tomorrow I would start the day with a fresh new chapter of life, going beyond the miseries of my past. In my heart I knew that life could only get better. Regardless of the outcome, the choices would be mine. The future was in my hands.

About the Author

Born in Beaumont, Texas the author has experienced many aspects of personal growth through a number of difficult situations. His employment background is as checkered as his childhood, and includes stints working as deckhand on a tug boat, construction labor, entertainer, salesman, heavy equipment operator, cowboy, truck driver, farmer, motel manager, miner, apartment manager, and private investigator.

For the past 25 years, Cliff and his lovely wife Elaine have made Idaho their home. They are the proud parents of two sons and a daughter; Robert, Timothy, and Misty. Doctors said there could be no children after Robert, but prayer and faith proved otherwise.

In 1985 Cliff became a reserve police officer, and knew he had found the career he had always searched for. A few years later he was hired full time. His previous experiences placed him in a unique position to thoroughly understand the needs of the community. He progressed through the ranks of corporal and sergeant until one of his proudest moments came in 1997 when he was appointed Chief of Police, a position he currently holds. As Cliff says, "If you have a dream and are willing to pay the price to see its fulfillment, there's nothing in the world that can stop you from achieving it."